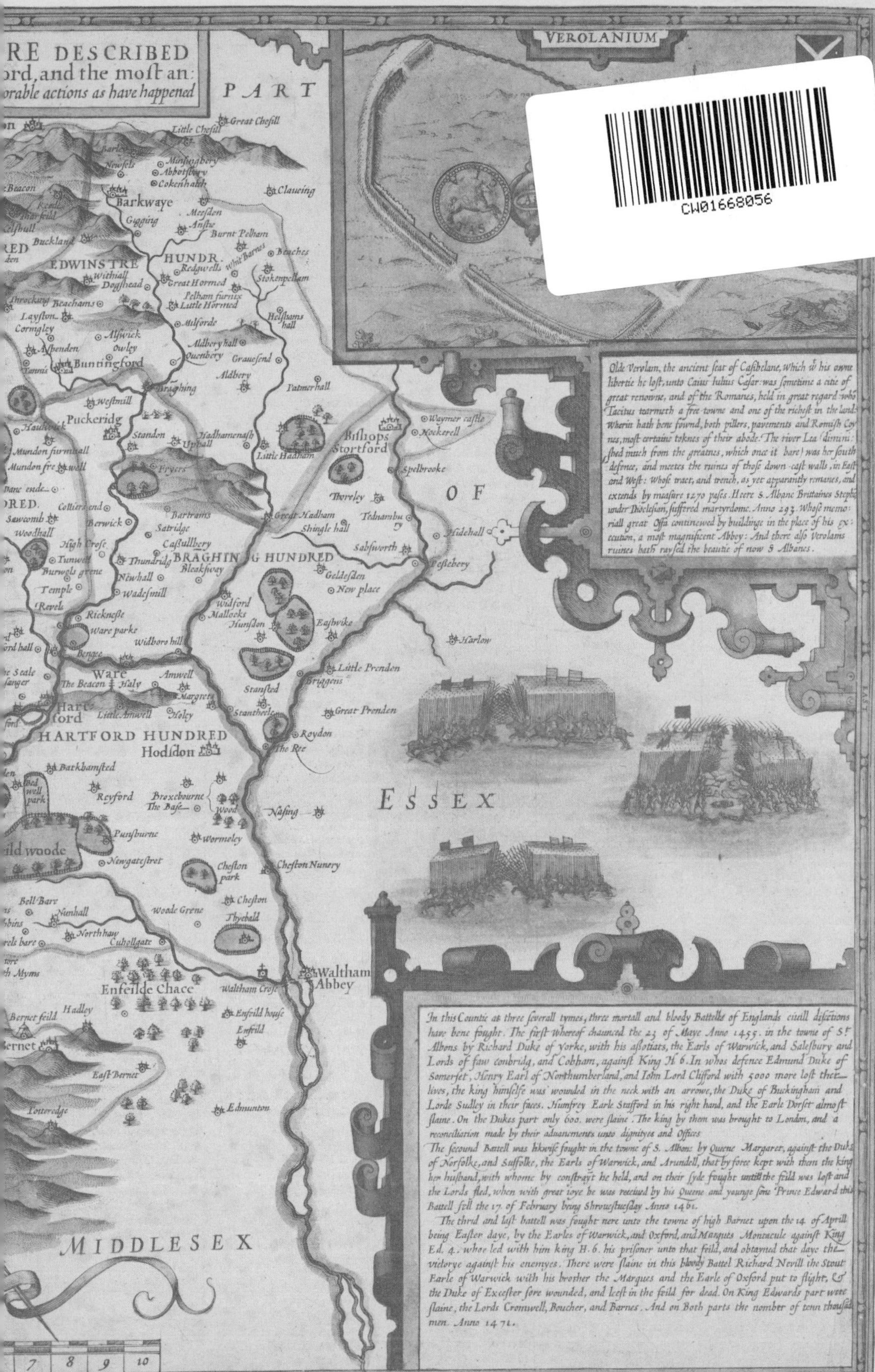
RE DESCRIBED
ord, and the most an:
orable actions as have happened
VEROLANIUM
PART
OF
ESSEX
MIDDLESEX
EDWINSTRE
HUNDR.
BRAGHING HUNDRED
HARTFORD HUNDRED
Barkwaye
Buntingford
Puckeridg
Bishops Stortford
Ware
Hartford
Hodsdon
Waltham Abbey
Enfeilde Chace
Great Chesill
Little Chesill
Claueing
Standon
Little Hadham
Great Hadham
Sabsworth
Harlow
Roydon
Nasing
Cheston Nunery
Enfeild
Edmunton
East Bernet
Hadley
7
8
9
10
Olde Verolam, the ancient seat of Casibelane, Which wt his owne libertie he lost, unto Caius Iulius Cesar: was sometime a citie of great renowne, and of the Romanes, held in great regard: who Tacitus tearmeth a free towne and one of the richest in the land: Wherin hath bene found, both pillers, pavements and Romish Coynes, most certaine toknes of their abode. The river Lea (diminished much from the greatnes, which once it bare) was her south defence, and meetes the ruines of those down-cast walls, in East and West: Whose tract, and trench, as yet apparantly remaines, and extends by measure 1270 pases. Heere S. Albane Brittaines Stephe under Dioclesian, suffered martyrdome. Anno 293. Whose memoriall great Offa continewed by buildinge in the place of his execution, a most magnificent Abbey: And there also Verolams ruines hath raysed the beautie of now S Albanes.
In this Countie at three severall tymes, three mortall and bloody Battells of Englands civill discetions have bene fought. The first whereof chaunced the 23 of Maye Anno 1455. in the towne of St Albons by Richard Duke of Yorke, with his assotiats, the Earls of Warwick, and Salesbury and Lords of faw conbridg, and Cobham, against King H. 6. In whos defence Edmund Duke of Somerset, Henry Earl of Northumberland, and Iohn Lord Clifford with 5000 more lost their lives, the king himselfe was wounded in the neck with an arrowe, the Duke of Buckingham and Lorde Sudley in their faces. Humfrey Earle Stafford in his right hand, and the Earle Dorset almost slaine. On the Dukes part only 600. were slaine. The king by them was brought to London, and a reconciliation made by their aduancements unto dignityes and Offices
The secound Battell was likewise fought in the towne of S. Albons by Queene Margaret, against the Duks of Norfolke, and Suffolke, the Earls of Warwick, and Arundell, that by force kept with them the king her husband, with whome by constrayt he held, and on their syde fought untill the feild was lost and the Lords fled, when with great ioye he was receiued by his Queene and younge sone Prince Edward this Battell fell the 17. of February being Shrowestuesday Anno 1461.
The third and last battell was fought nere unto the towne of high Barnet upon the 14 of Aprill being Easter daye, by the Earles of Warwick, and Oxford, and Marques Montacule against King Ed. 4. whoe led with him king H. 6. his prisoner unto that feild, and obtayned that daye the victorye against his enemyes. There were slaine in this bloody Battel Richard Nevill the Stout Earle of Warwick with his brother the Marques and the Earle of Oxford put to flight, & the Duke of Excester sore wounded, and leeft in the feild for dead. On King Edwards part were slaine, the Lords Cromwell, Boucher, and Barnes. And on Both parts the nomber of tenn thousād men. Anno 1471.

HERTFORDSHIRE YESTERDAYS

HERTFORDSHIRE YESTERDAYS

FRANK BALLIN
MALCOLM TOMKINS

Kylin Press

First published in the United Kingdom 1982
by the Kylin Press Limited
Darbonne House · Waddesdon · Buckinghamshire

ISBN 0 907128 06 8

Designed by Peter Tucker · Oxford
Typeset by Kylin typesetting · Oxford
Printed by Sawtells · Sherborne · Dorset

Contents

Introduction

MALCOLM TOMKINS, greatly talented as a local historian, was a rare person in our time with an interest in antiquities for what they could contribute to knowledge for its own sakc, and in the best tradition of parson-gentleman scholars, for whom trouble and effort in original research were a cost never counted. An able writer, one of Malcolm Tomkins' great interests was the people who lived in Hertfordshire, though himself of retiring nature.

Frank Ballin, however, is widely known for his many years active contribution to the public and political life of Hertfordshire. He has researched and written of past stories in mid-Hertfordshire, to the greater interest — and pleasure — of two generations and more of Hertfordshire people.

Frank Ballin's writings are notable for their attractive popularisation of the subject of local history and respect for traditional English values, for the careful reconstruction of the stories of historic houses, and for the historical background of colourful local characters and tales standing at the threshold of legend.

Dr. Doris Jones — Baker F.S.A.

ACKNOWLEDGEMENTS

The publishers would like to thank the County Archivist and his staff, and the Barnet and St. Albans museums, for their help in providing illustrations. Over the years both Frank Ballin and Malcolm Tomkins have written extensively in the *Hertfordshire Countryside* magazine and we would like to thank Mr. E. V. Scott, the Editor, for agreeing to these articles being published.

Strange old maps

TO COME across one of the early maps of the county is to find yourself looking at a Hertfordshire countryside altogether strange. It is a countryside — seemingly — of mountain wastes and trackless plains, of lonely church towers and isolated miniature, red, pinnacled towns.

But that, of course, is not a true picture of the Elizabethan and Jacobean Hertfordshire which the maps profess to portray. The contemporary traveller knew well enough that roads, however bad they were, did cross the county — just as he knew better than to be unduly daunted by the complex mountain systems that, to judge by the maps, stretched across the north and the south; for these represent nothing more formidable than the gently rising land that is Hertfordshire's share in the Chilterns and the series of comparatively low ridges between Barnet and Rickmansworth.

Outside these mountain ranges the hills take on the semblance of monstrous sugar-loaves, painted brown or green at the whim of the colourist. On the summits of those at Amwell, Graveley and Therfield stand the tall, pylon-like beacons that played their part in an alarm system which lasted until the time of the Commonwealth. But even these beacon hills were never the impressive vantage points that the maps make them look.

If, however, the hills are on the steep side, the rivers very happily suggest the unhurried meanderings of our Hertfordshire streams — even though a certain waywardness in their serpentine bends betrays that fact that this is fortuitous. Equally so is the way the church towers are, one and all, crowned with a Hertfordshire 'spike', for these are no more than conventional signs, doing service for the villages clustering round them in the same way that the little clumps of green trees represent whole woodlands.

Many of these are fenced off by realistically drawn palings in a green park. Of these, Hatfield was the largest even on the earliest map — Christopher Saxton's of 1577 — when Queen Elizabeth's Oak lay on its outermost edge; and it can be seen to have annexed the neighbouring woods by the time of Robert Morden's map of 1695. On this, too, appeared such parks as Astridg (*sic*), Balls and Knebworth Place, which had not been shown at all on previous maps; and while it is true that others, such as Theobalds, had disappeared, and that yet others, like Sopwell, had already vanished on John Speede's map of 1611, the picture none the less emerges of a Hertfordshire landscape increasingly dotted with parks.

But they did not appear, as soon as they were enclosed, on each successive map which followed Speede's, because for many years this was merely reprinted or copied. No new survey was made when the two great Dutch printing houses of Bleau and Jansson published their highly artistic versions in the 1640s, nor when Richard Blome brought out his much less elegant little map in 1673. All were content to reproduce the details on Speede's map, which, incidentally, had also been printed in Holland.

There is, however, one feature on Speede's map which is on no other: inset in the corners are prospects of 'Hartford and the most ancient towne S. Albons.' The one of the county town gives a picture of it, down to the last house, as it must have looked three and a half centuries ago. The same cannot altogether be said of St. Albans, where — alongside its 'most magnificent Abbey' — 'St Albane' can be seen kneeling, with hands clasped beneath the upraised sword by which he 'suffered martyrdome Anno 293,' and where only the abbey and one other church — perhaps St. Peter's — stand out from what is otherwise a mere jumble of roofs.

This vagueness as to detail is a weakness no less of the map itself. 'Shepeshide,' for instance, is alike misplaced and misspelt — though it is not as oddly spelt as the 'Cambelow Grenh' on Bleau's map. The Dutch printer was not to know what a green was or that this 'Hertfordshire' abounded in them; and lack of such knowledge as he attempted to copy Speede's map multiplied its errors.

It was not until the end of the century, with the publication of Morden's map, that any attempt was made 'to supply the defects, rectifie the positions, and correct the false spellings.' Here — though not for the very first time — the main roads were inserted and the changes which had altered the face of the county during the century were incorporated. Thus 'Mackrill End' makes its first appearance. I wonder if this can have been the map which Lamb had in mind when he wrote of 'Mackery End; or Mackerel End, as it is spelt, perhaps more properly, in some old maps of Hertfordshire' — though his reason for supposing that this might be spelling it more properly is puzzling, for the place is reputed to be named after one John Machary.

Be that as it may, some of the names on Morden's map are, in a sense, spelt 'more properly' than at first might appear. 'Berkhamsted, Cudicot, Fresden, Gadsden, Hodsdon, Kelshull, Punsburn, Tharfield and Wimbley' echo the pronunciation of the day. Some of these forms indeed have survived, though others are either dying or already as dead as the 'Sabesworth' and 'Yardley' on John Norden's map of 1607.

On Norden's map, too, allowance has to be made for the interchanging of the letters U and V. It can be seen in 'Vphall' and, conversely, in 'Bigraue' and 'Graueley' as well as in a note of 'A Battel wher the danes were overthrown.'

'In memoriall of their overthrow,' records Norden in the notes accompanying his map of 1598, 'the place where the fight was is to this day called Dane End,' and on the map itself it is marked by two badly depleted armies, bristling with swords and fighting hand to hand, while similar mimic skirmishes rage at Barnet and St. Albans. Speede, on his map, contents himself with pitching camp at 'Bernet field' and St. Albans, only drawing up the opposing forces of York and Lancaster for one 'St. Albans Battaill' of the two which that city has seen. Outside the map, however, all 'three mortall and bloody Battells' are described in detail and illustrated on a larger scale, the close phalanx of lances dipping into the attack looking deceptively, at first glance, like nothing so much as a field of corn falling before the onslaught of a band of harvesters — an image which seems indeed not inappropriate to 'this fine corn county.'

But its excellence in this and other respects does not go by unrecognized. 'The aire,' notes Speede on the back of his map, 'is temperate, sweet, and healthfull, as seated in a Climate neither too hot, nor too cold: the soil is rich, plentious, and delightfull, yeelding abundance of Corne, Cattle, Wood, and Grasse, destitute of nothing that ministreth profit or pleasures for life.'

And this might seem to be the theme of some of the embellishments to the borders of the maps. On Bleau's, an emblematic sheaf is borne in the arms of one who may well be the great Ceres herself, crowned as she is with a chaplet of corn

Sᵀ. ALBAN'S.

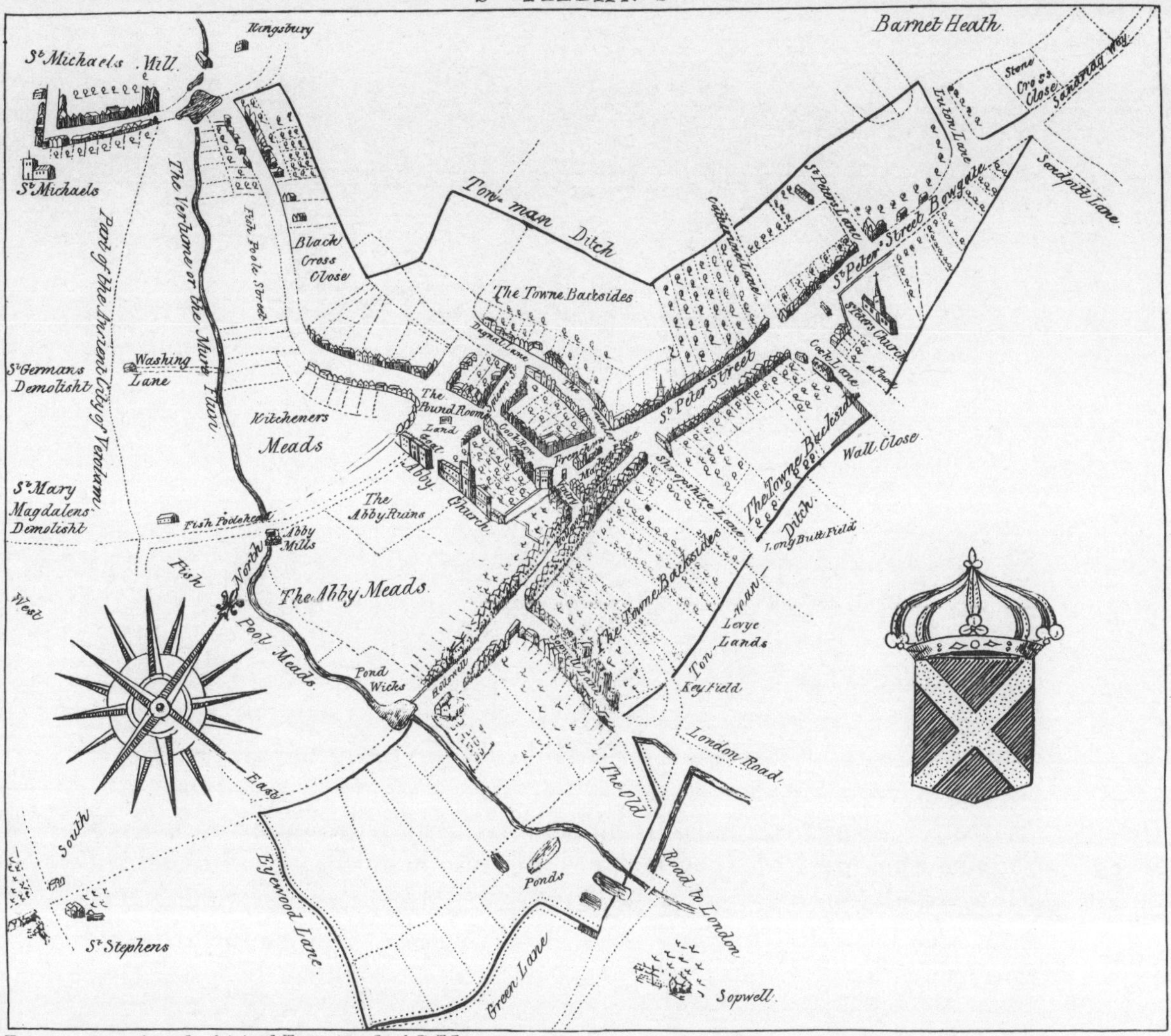

F. Ballin

Drawn on Stone from the Original Engravings by C. L. Tyler.

and attired in such unpractically flowing robes; while two stray ears, of distinctly bedraggled appearance, are brandished by an attendant cherub. It is left to Jansson to complete the picture of Arcadian plenty with his shepherd swain keeping a vigilant eye less on his flock than on two nymphs gleaning, and his pair of bucolic little boys, one wielding a flail white the other pipes a rustic tune.

But it would be fanciful to suppose that these pretty pastoral figures bear much relation to the real Hertfordshire. They belong to that idyllic world dear to the imagination of the time — denizens of those sunlit mountains which exist only in the picturesque Hertfordshire of these old maps.

Thomas Baskerville

EARLY TRAVELLER

AMONG the earliest travellers' impressions of Hertfordshire are those of Thomas Baskerville, who left a composite account of several journeys he made at different times through the county. The first of them took place 300 years ago: September 24, 1671, found him in Watford, bound for St. Albans but reining his horse in at the sight of the swollen waters of the River Colne that lay across his road. Reckoning that he would not be able to get across without the water rising as high as the saddle on his horse, he eventually turned him about and 'went another way to St. Albans.'

This town, in a curious half-finished verse listing the attributes of various places he associated with 'straw tankards and pots'; but, from his own observation when he stayed there in 1681, what he noted was that a great deal of timber was bought and sold and that there were 'gates for highways ready-made to be sold.' These cannot at this date have been tollgates, but were presumably gates to stop traffic encroaching on the land adjoining the road, as it might be tempted to do if the mud was deep.

He could not fail to notice, too, the large number of inns in St. Albans, and he remarked 'The Bull inn is the greatest that I have seen in England.' Yet of this great establishment, which stood in Holywell Hill north of Sopwell Lane, not a trace remains. He himself stayed not there but at the Red Lion in Cook Row, as George Street was then called, and from his landlady, Mrs. Sellioke and her son he learnt much about the town. 'It hath four churches,' he recorded, referring of course to St. Peter's, St. Stephen's, St. Michael's and the abbey church, the last 'being an ancient old fabric and now much decayed.' That very year, however, he was told 'they are gathering money by the encouragement of the present Bishop

St. Albans as it would have appeared to Thomas Baskerville *M. Tomkins*

of London.' Whatever the response may have been, the abbey was to remain in a sorry state until the 19th century. As for its past, ''Twas built,' he learnt, 'by Offa, king of Mercia, in honour of that saint martyred by the emperor Diocletian, and in succeeding ages he had there a shrine . . . but in the days when popery was turned out of this land it was taken down and carried to France.' In telling Baskerville this, Master Sellioke was voicing a persistent local tradition that the Benedictines had snuggled the saint's relics out of the country, which is possible though there are no facts to substantiate it.

From Mrs. Sellioke Baskerville learnt that 'her well was 40 fathoms deep.' Deep wells, it was explained to him, were necessary in the upper parts of the town, though there 'is a small river running by the lower parts.' This, of course, was the Ver, which derived its name from the Roman Verulamium beside which it ran. 'Anciently a city,' it was in Baskerville's time — or so he wrote — 'a village'; perhaps he had St. Michael's in mind. From Verulam 'Lord Bacon had his title'; his 'great house' had lately been 'taken down and sold.' This was his ingenious summer house' (as John Aubrey called it) at Pondyards, which had been demolished in 1663.

In May 1681 Baskerville entered Hertfordshire on the Old North Road at Royston, 'a fair town with a great market for corn'; and here he 'went out of London Road, thwarting the fields under the brows of the hills in Hertfordshire.' On his way he noticed 'a hare-warren lately made and railed in by the present Earl of Salisbury,' and when he reached Baldock the landlord of his inn there told him that because many had escaped 'they were now very plentiful in the fields hereabout.' The Landlord also informed him that the town was 'so called from the scarcity of oaks' and, by way of proof, told him that there was 'now but one in the parish.' Oddly enough, although this unlikely deviation is not the generally accepted one that Baldock is a form of Baghdad it is echoed in a suggestion recently put forward that oaks were scarce enough hereabouts for one to be a landmark and that Baldock meant Bald (or round) Oak. From Baldock Baskerville travelled along the line of the Chilterns, which he described as a 'range of mountains,' and left the county, bound for Dunstable.

In September of the same year (1681) Baskerville visited the Earl of Bridgewater's 'great house' at Ashridge. 'Formerly some monastery' — in point of fact the College of Bonhommes — it was 'remarkable . . . for having in paint

Ashridge House, south face

Hertfordshire Record Office

upon the walls some scripture and monkish stories.' It stood 'on the plain of the hill four miles above Tring' and boasted 'a park for fallows and another for red deer, and in them especially near his house such lofty groves of trees and so thick set together that the like is scarce anywhere else to be seen; which conspiring to keep out the sunbeams makes the ground under them . . . as bare as a barn floor without grass.' He was told that 'Lord Chancellor Hyde coming hither one time to visit the present earl found fault because it had so much wood about it,' but Baskerville reckoned it was a wise policy to retain this, for 'doubtless were it not for these trees this would in the winter-time be a very sharp cold place, standing as it doth so high and open to all the northern storms.' They were certainly appreciated by the squirrels (red, of course) that he watched in large numbers 'leap from tree to tree.'

Baskerville went through a gatehouse that led to the stables and, there, in a quadrangle, saw a deep well worked by a horse 'in a great wheel.' This must have been the old monastery well, which still exists and is 300 feet deep. The water was drawn up in two large buckets, 'a man always standing by as soon as the bucket comes above the collar of the well to empty it into a leaden cisterns; and here,' added Baskerkerville, 'the ingenuity of the horse must not be forgotten, for as soon as the man lays hold of the bucket to empty it, the horse turns himself in the wheel without bidding and travels the other way to draw up the next bucket.' By the well was a pond, into which the water was run after it had served the house and which contained 'some few hungry carp.'

Another gatehouse led 'through a large court on the northern side of the house to which they ascend by steps on a terrace-walk.' The hall Baskerville found a noble room, with life-sized pictures of 'good horses which my lord hath been the owner of' and 'a fair shuffleboard table' which he had had made from an ash tree lately cut down on his estate. Baskerville went on to explore the buttery, 'adorned with many heads and horns of stage of red deer which have been killed out of my lord's own park' and the cellars — which were probably the crypt of the monastery — where the household beer was made on a scale that used six pounds of hops at a brewing! Nor did he miss the 'fine gardens about the house . . . in the park a neat lodgehouse, and a little without the park in the way towards Tring a good country alehouse.'

In the following year he set out on a journey to St. Albans with his man, entering Hertfordshire this time in the southwest corner 'through the pleasant

An early engraving of St. Albans Abbey

M. Tomkins

bottoms of this country.' This was the Chiltern countryside around Chenies, whence — by 'hills . . . shaded with beech, oak and birch' — he reached 'Rickmanstead,' as he called Rickmansworth. 'A pretty little market town' he found it, admiring too 'upon a hill on the other side the stream' Moor Park. 'Marching forward a mile or two more,' he reached 'Casabell' — by which he meant Cashiobury — and then, by way of Watford, St. Albans.

In the abbey — on this occasion or another — he saw the alleged tomb of 'an ancient British traveller,' Sir John Manderville, having in the roof of the church over his body these verses for an epitaph:

Loe is this Inn of travel doth lye
One rich in nothing but a memorye

Now, three centuries later, Thomas Baskerville himself ranks as 'an ancient English traveller,' but — unlike Sir John's fantastic accounts of his travels — every word that Thomas Baskerville wrote smacks of the truth and tells us much about the Hertfordshire through which he travelled.

Ancient Manor of Hatfield Woodhall

THE POSSESSIONS of the great family of Cecil include various sub-manors, which in time became merged in the main manor of Hatfield. Among these was Hatfield Woodhall, situated to the east of the Great North Road between Mill Green and Stanborough. According to Chauncy, who wrote his *Historical Antiquities of Hertfordshire* towards the end of the seventeenth century, its name was derived from the great abundance of timber in the district, which was indeed a characteristic of the greater part of Hertfordshire in the olden days.

Its first recorded tenants were the Bassingburnes, who in the time of Edward I held the manor of the main manor of Hatfield by the service of half a knight's fee, suit of court and the yearly rent of 2d. In the troubled times of the fourteenth century, when the king was often away from home at the French wars, there was very little control over the activities of the more lawless of the landed gentry. We read that about the period of the Black Death, Stephen de Bassingbourne complained that William de Ludwick, with his sons John and Thomas, tenants of another sub-manor of Hatfield, 'broke his close and house in Bishops Hatfield, entered his free warren, carried away his goods and hares, rabbits, pheasants and partridges from the warren and assaulted his servants.' We have not been able to trace the outcome of Stephen's complaint, or whether it was justified.

In the reign of Elizabeth I the manor came into the possession of the family of Boteler, another branch of which owned Watton Woodhall in the neighbourhood of Watton-at-stone. The manor was also called Woodhall for the same reason as its namesake at Hatfield. Sir John Boteler, lord of the manor of Hatfield Woodhall in the early part of the seventeenth century, was one of the earliest recipients of the title of baronet after the institution of this rank by James I, and by Charles I was advanced to the peerage under the style of Lord Boteler of Brandfield. His wife was Elizabeth Villiers, eldest sister of the first Duke of Buckingham of that family, famous as a favourite of our first two Stuart kings.

William, the only one of his sons who survived him, was an idiot from birth, and at his death the peerage of Boteler of Brandfield became extinct, the lordship of Hatfield Woodhall passing to Francis Boteler, the son of Ralph Boteler of Tewin Hall. Sir Francis is eulogized by Chauncy as a fine example of the smaller country gentleman, who formed the backbone of English parliaments in the Stuart period. He served under the unfortunate Earl of Strafford in the Irish troubles, and on the outbreak of the civil war was returned to England to join the King's forces and soon afterwards received the honour of knighthood from King Charles at York.

A story used to be told in the neighbourhood that Sir Francis was wont periodically to ride his horse up the steps of Hatfield House and so right through the armoury to the south side, for he claimed that the mansion had been erected

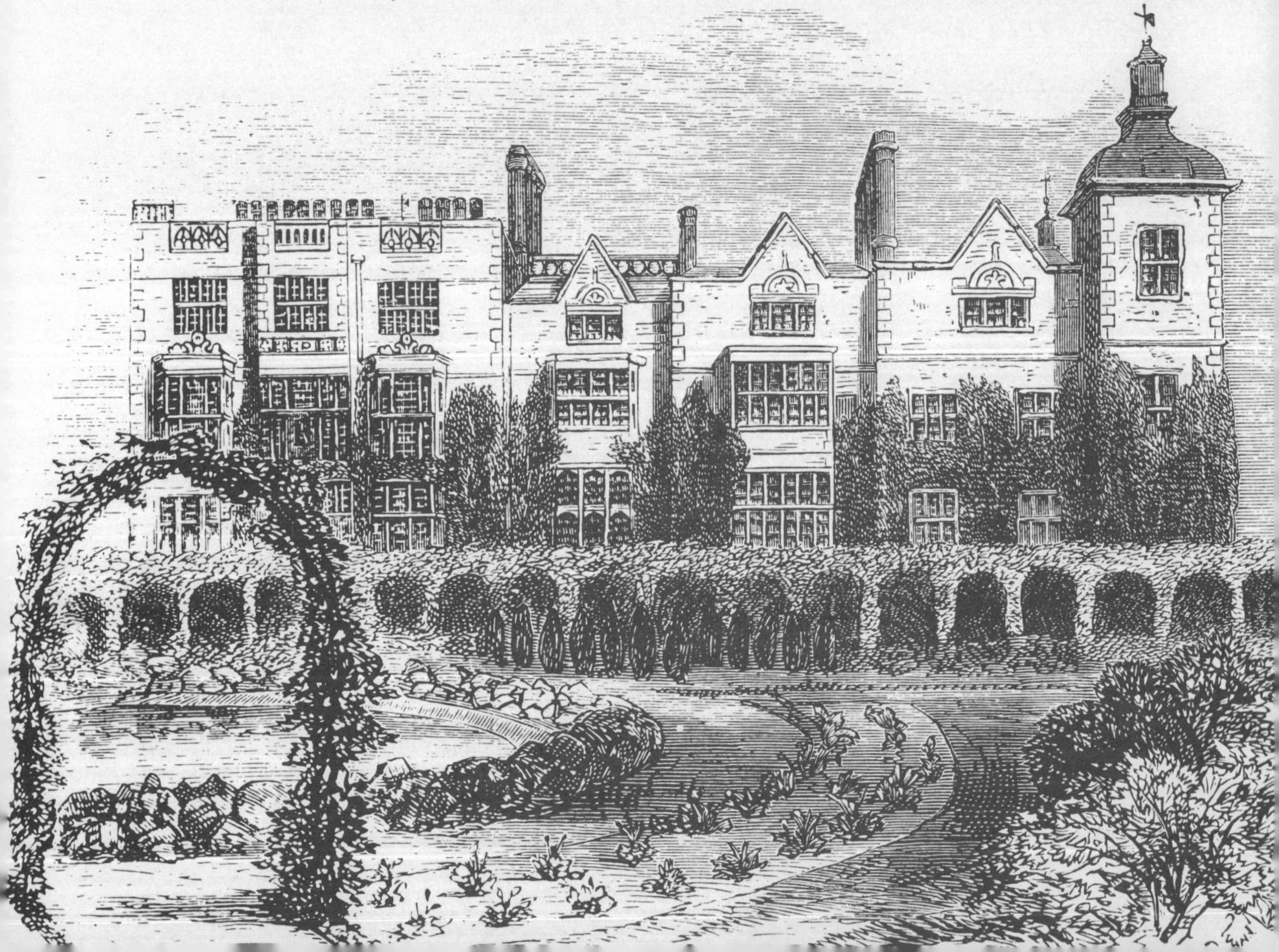

over a bridle path, which he said should never be closed to him. If this tale be true, one wonders what were the consequent reactions of the Earl of Salisbury of the period! In 1678 he conveyed a farm, called Clarkes or Leggs, in Ludwick Hyde to trustees and provided that the rents and profits of this farm should be for ever equally divided among four poor widows of Hatfield and one of Tewin. He died in 1690 and, his only son, George, having predeceased him, his elder daughter, Julia, widow of Francis Shallcross of Digswell, became the lady of the manor of Hatfield Woodhall. On her death the manor came to her sister Isabella, the widow of Charles Hutchinson of Owthorpe in the county of Nottingham, who lived to the great age of ninety-one. The manor remained in the possession of this family until 1792, when the Rev. Julius Hutchinson sold it to James Cecil, first Marquess of Salisbury, and thus Hatfield Woodhall became merged in the manor paramount of Hatfield. The marquess is said to have disliked having such a fine mansion in the neighbourhood of Hatfield House, which it rivalled in splendour, and when shortly afterwards part of the house was burnt down he caused most of the remaining portion to be demolished.

At a later date a farmhouse was erected on part of the site of the old manor house, and this in its turn was also destroyed by fire and was eventually replaced by a modern building, tenanted by Mrs. C.J. Noad, who farms the adjoining land. It is pleasant to record that what remains of the old manor house is again inhabited and is now the home of Mr. & Mrs. Peter J. Timson, Mrs. Noad's son-in-law and daughter, to whom great credit is due for its present excellent state of preservation. Above a window on the south side can be seen the coat of arms of the Hutchinson family, bearing the date 1785.

At Hatfield House there can yet be seen two relics of Hatfield Woodhall. One of these is a beautiful wrought-iron gate which now leads into the east garden. On the upper portion of the gate can be seen the monogram F.B. (the initials of Sir Francis Boteler), intertwined with oak-leaves and acorns. The other is the Renaissance doorway to Woodhall, bearing over it a shield quartered with the Boteler arms, which has been re-erected in the east garden overlooking the new Pond.

Let us conclude with an expression of thankfulness that this relic of a bygone age still stands within walking distance of two of our most extensive new towns and express the hope that it may long continue to serve its present useful function.

James Ripley, Barnet ostler and author

THE RED LION inn at the top of Barnet Hill was rebuilt in the 1930's replacing one that had stood there for over two centuries. A far larger establishment this, in the 18th century it had provided stabling for over a hundred horses — enough, one would think, to keep its ostlers on the go. But one of them — James Ripley — found time to write letters to the papers; indeed, when it came to letter-writing, he seems to have been unable to hold his horses! And so proud was he of the effusions of his pen that in 1781 he published them under the title: *Select Original Letters on Various Subjects by James Ripley* now, and for thirty years past. *Ostler at the Red Lion, Barnet.*

The book was dedicated to the Royal Regiment of Horse Guards Blue in 'grateful acknowledgement for the generous encouragement I always received from you, for my unmerited services in the stable.' And he assured them: 'I shall always esteem it an honour to rub down your horses' heels so long as I am able to stoop. . .'

Stoop he might as an ostler, but rise he felt confident he would as a writer. Had he not the testimony of A Friend to Merit, whose verse 'addressed to J. Ripley, Ostler' on April 18, 1775, he quoted in his book? It finishes:

So may you rise, and with just fame excel,
And your chief glory be in writing well.

St. Albans Museum

The frontispiece to James Ripley's book, showing him writing in the Red Lion at Barnet

Our illustration depicts Ripley surrounded by the tools of both his trades — ostler and author, the first represented by such articles as a sieve and a curry-comb, the second by quill pens and paper. He is seated apparently in the Red Lion, which was also Barnet's post office, for the words '*Post Office*' appear on the door behind him. The adjacent pigeon-holes were presumably used for sorting the mail but in the picture are stacked with copies of the *Whitehall Evening*

Post, the *Craftsman* and the *Gazetteer* — presumably three of the papers which he had favoured with his letters.

And what were they about? They include advice to his son and a proposal of marriage to one whom he hoped he might call 'by the tender and endearing name of Mrs. R — y' but mostly are on subjects that arose from his employment as an ostler, which seems to have left him with more respect for horses than for many of his fellow human beings. 'No man endowed with humanity,' he wrote, 'but must feel compassion for his horse, when he sees him come limping out of the stable upon three legs, at the same time that perhaps he has a journey to perform of some hundred miles.' This was partly the fault of the groom, for 'nothing is more practised by a set of my ignorant brethren when a gentleman alights at the inn, than advising him to have his horses' heels washed (or rather daubed) out with pot-liquor,' Ripley recommended instead a mash, a turnip poultice and blood-letting; he had no more time for 'those itinerant quacks, who trudge through the streets with a melting ladle and gally-pot, filled with horse-turpentine.'

The chief culprits, however, in reducing the horses to this pitiable state were that 'new species of gentry yclept post-boys,' than whom 'no set of men have arrived to such a degree of impudence, debrauchery, and extravagance.' They were encouraged in this 'by the masters of little waggon and hogg-inns,' who bribed 'those tender conscienced gentry (the post-boys) . . . to affirm that they have the best horses and chaise that is to be met with upon the road.' Ripley would have liked to see 'every post-boy, who has the insolence to direct noblemen &c. where to take horses' paid with 'a good horsewhip'.

Perhaps this letter it was that appeared in *The Craftsman*, where Ripley imagined a post-boy reading just such a one to his cronies: 'Jack English cries out, 'Zounds, lads, there is a letter in the Craftsman that deserves to be burned by the common hangman . . . The writer . . . must be some pitiful low-lifed mechanic, or musty growling tradesman . . . but . . . we gentlemen of the whip have more refined tastes; a rump-steak cannot be relished by us without oyster sauce, and the wing of a goose is insipid without apple-sauce; in short we expect to be treated with the most elegant viands and richest liquors the inn affords . . . As long as the generous inn-keeper continues to treat us in this manner, and tip us a couple of shillings to get drunk in going home, we will exert ourselves to prevail upon noblemen and gentlemen to call at his house. You may easily judge of our consequence when I inform you we very often receive four, five or six shillings back carriage . . . Perhaps we are censured for abusing our masters' horses . . . Some ill-natured masters have come to the resolution to discharge us, but they are always treated with contempt by all the respectable fraternity of post-boys . . . We can easily furnish ourselves at a livery-stable with a nimble footed horse, and procure a brace of pistols, and act MacHeath upon Hounslow heath or Finchley common, and make our exit in an elevated situation.' Presumably this was an allusion to the gallows, the destination of most highwaymen.

Ripley was determined to blacken the post-boys' name; but there is no doubt that he was not maligning them when he accused them of taking bribes. This corruption of the local boys lasted into the next century, for William Kitchener recounted in 1828 how he had fared at the hands of one of them: 'A Post Boy . . . had been told by his Master I was going the North Road. At Barnet I fixed on my own house to be driven to, at which he seemed surprised: I told him also I had determined to go the Low, not the High North Road. He expressed great concern at hearing the alteration I had made in my route; and on my inquiring the reason, he candidly told me it would make a difference to him of half a guinea, for had I allowed him to take me to their own house, as he termed it, or that to which he was in the habit of driving, and I had continued on the High North Road, he should have received that sum from the Landlord, as a gratuity for taking him the Fare, a perquisite which would be repaid him by a charge made to the Post Masters generally on that road.'

But to return to Ripley: the reason for his own grievance appears in another letter. 'I reside,' he wrote, 'in a great thoroughfare town, not more than twelve miles from London (Barnet, of course) in which are several capital inns, and I have the honour to be employed by the master of one of them (the Red Lion), to whom a few days ago I took the liberty to present my bill.' This was for his wages; but his master told him 'it was not in his power to pay me; that he had an execution in the house, and that I might think myself happy if I got two shillings in the pound.' And the reason? — his employer's money had been 'wantonly lavished away amongst a set of wretches who are a disgrace to the human species; I mean the London post-boys.'

His improvident employer must have been William Broughton, landlord of the Red Lion and postmaster of Barnet from 1772 to 1788, in which year a print was published showing this inn with *Post Office* over the door, *Neat Post Chaise*

FOOTBALL, Played at the Market Place, Barnet.

Barnet Museum

Red Lion as Ripley knew it, when William Broughton was the landlord and post master

above the sign and *Wm. Broughton* beneath it. As well as being publican and postmaster, he was — like many another inn-keeper of his day — a farmer. Ripley described his farm as 'very extensive:' and after walking round it one May morning he wrote: 'as I have near thirty years been confined to attend the stables and yard, a kind of new world was opened to my view.' He heard the 'melodious lark' and the cuckoo — a bird which he was not alone among his contemporaries in believing fed upon other birds' eggs and, later in the year, turned into a hawk!

As a nature correspondent he was not in the first rank; as an observer of men and manners at the Red Lion he is much more reliable. He was stern on the subject of 'those nimble-fingered gentlemen who leave specimens of their wit or folly, in trying the goodness of their diamond upon the glass-windows of every place they visit.' This arduous method of indulging a taste for graffiti was, it seems, much practised by our ancestors; and — if James Ripley is to be believed

— 'curiosity often draws the fair sex to the window in expectation of meeting with some innocent piece of wit, or quotation from some eminent author; but how cruel the disappointment when she finds some indecent allusion, or downright obscenity!'

Of the fop who travelled abroad Ripley thought little, reckoning that the only advantage it gave him was that 'he will be able at his return to convince his dull countrymen that he has made some interesting improvements in the cock of his hat, the tying of his cravat or sword knot, &c.'

The 'carters, waggoners, coachmen, and masters of post-chaises' he criticised for over-weighting their fore-wheels and declared his intention 'to have a waggon in miniature of such construction as shall prove the weight exactly.'

Ripley himself did not take kindly to criticism; and when he encountered in the St. James evening paper a letter addressed to him 'in a dull and laboured irony, congratulating me upon my happy genius as a writer of moral essays,' he responded with a letter of the most threatening order. He informed his critic that he would like to have been able to have 'seized you by both ears . . . and given your loggerhead forty-five severe knocks against the pavement . . . without endangering your skull, as nature has sufficiently fortified you against accidents of this kind. After this I would have stripped you naked, tied both your hands together with a strong halter to one of the stable posts, and given you the discipline of the horse whip.'

From this 'moral essay' it is a relief to turn to another, in which he recorded having seen 'a new species of gambling exhibited upon Barnet common.' Large bets were placed on 'a young gentleman's riding two miles upon a full gallop, standing upright in the stirrups,' on which Ripley's comment was that 'though his activity might recommend him as a pupil at Sadler's Wells, yet it is below a Gentleman.'

Indeed, he did not approve of racehorses at all and would have liked to see them taxed out of existence: this, he reckoned, would 'reduce the price of oats' and 'afford more pasturage for sheep and oxen: then,' he went on, waxing Biblical in his enthusiasm, 'will the mountains be covered with sheep, and the valleys with oxen . . . and the flesh of both may then be eaten by thousands who have long been unaccustomed to such delicious food.' A happy thought, even if time has proved there to have been a fallacy somewhere in James Ripley's economics.

The Mill House at Welwyn

IN MEDIEVAL ENGLAND when the great bulk of the population was engaged in purely agricultural pursuits, people were self-supporting to a degree unimaginable in these days of mass production and easy communication with the most isolated districts. As they lacked food to give their cattle in the winter, families used to kill them in the autumn and salt them down for their own winter food. In addition they used to brew their own beer and bake their own bread. It is the latter aspect of medieval life that concerns us here, because in the matter of grinding their corn they were subject to the customs of the manor, where they dwelt. The lords of the manor often insisted that their tenants should take their corn to be ground at the manorial mill and retained a proportion of their corn as a fee for this purpose.

This obligation often caused friction between the lord of the manor and his tenants and was one of the chief causes of the peasants' revolt in 1381 when the abbot of St. Albans levied this unwelcome charge upon his tenants, many of whom could well grind their corn in their own homes.

Thus we can see that from the earliest times mills were an important item in the country's economy. Some were worked by wind-power and others by water and as the sites of villages were often chosen for their proximity to water, there was usually a suitable river to afford the necessary power to operate a water mill.

In these days of large combines which process the grain in bulk, the need for a mill in every town and village has constantly declined, which accounts for the very small number now left in actual operation.

In Hertfordshire in 1855 there were 82 millers and seven millwrights, but by

1965 the numbers of mills still in existence had declined to 14, of which only three were still occasionally worked. Today there are none.

Tradition has it that our little river Mimram or Maran supplied power for a mill at Welwyn since the time of the Conquest and this continued to be worked until the early years of the present century.

The first recorded miller was William Attendene in 1290. The late Branch Johnson, in the first of his two very informative books about Welwyn, tells us about a curious example of payment by kind in the old days. In 1427 William Redhede was granted by the rector a lease for ten years and a sub-tenant of his, William Sybern, had to pay a premium for his admission of a trout and an eel. Verily the Mimram in those days must have been a paradise for anglers.

Records for the intervening centuries are scanty, but the Welwyn Mill is definitely listed as belonging to the manor of the Rectory in 1461. In 1469 we are told that Thomas Dene of Montfichet, otherwise Ayot St. Peter or Little Ayot 'Broke and entered it to the rector's damage.' Presumably the historians of old were only interested in recording untoward incidents, because two years later we read that Thomas Payn the miller was fined for obstructing the millstream and causing it to overflow the king's highway.

In February, 1795, there was a severe frost in Welwyn, which was followed by a sudden thaw. The River Mimram overflowed its banks and passed through the rectory garden flooding the ground floors of several houses in Mill Lane and the adjacent streets. The flood water passed through the mill, where it carried away some outhouses and in the stable two of the miller's horses narrowly escaped drowning.

Some 70 years ago a tragedy occurred in the mill pond where a boy was drowned. This pond was drained in 1905 and there is now a lawn on the site. In former times a barn ran across the Mimram to the site of the present garage, but this was pulled down some years later.

Welwyn Mill is listed in Domesday as liable for taxation purposes under Mardleybury and this must refer to a small part of the land to the east of the actual mill as the boundary between the manor of Mardleybury and the manor of the rectory lay in the vicinity of what is now Mill Lane.

It is not until the early years of the 18th century that we can trace the name of another occupant of the mill. This was Nicholas Ludford, recorded as the miller

Overleaf/The Mill House in the early 20th Century/Dr. & Mrs. Abrahams

in 1724. He was also the keeper of the toll-gate. Some thirty years later in the time of his successors relict, the Widow Smith or that of Evans, who followed her, the greater part of the present Mill House was built which until 1850 spanned the river.

It is interesting to note that we have definite proof of the rebuilding of the house in the middle of the 18th century, because a bricklayer has left his initials E.P. with the date 1754 on a brick in the wall facing the river. When Dr. and Mrs. Sisson had some alterations made to this wall and a new window added 200 years later their bricklayer inscribed his initials C.P. with the date 1954 on another brick. As these two bricks are in close proximity, one can well imagine that these two dates so close together may well give food for thought for future historians.

There was apparently nothing else of especial interest to record about Welwyn Mill after it was rebuilt in 1754, because with the exception of John Patmore, who succeeded Evans, we cannot trace the names of any later millers until we come to the last one of all. This was James Chalkley, who came from a long line of millers and who died in 1912. This name appears in the Welwyn Church registers at various times in the 18th century but we cannot trace any connection with the mill.

May I say here that if any of our readers have any records of some of the millers in the intervening period it would help us to complete the story of one of the few mills in Hertfordshire that was still working in the present century.

William Jenkins, whose son lives nearby at Welwyn, was a man of short stature and possessed of remarkable strength. He was an employee of James Chalkley and his son recalled that with his bare hands he could lift sacks of flour weighing 2¼ cwt. His principal job was to hack the mill stones and to make them rough after they had been worn smooth. This task he performed by using a chisel and hitting this with a hammer.

After the death of James Chalkley the actual mill was demolished and the chimney at the south end of the house taken down.

The mill had been long comprised within the manor of Lockleys and after the death of George Dering, who was far famed for his scientific interests and inventions, Mill House was sold by his daughter, Mrs. Rosa Georgina Neall.

In 1914 Wilfred Arthur Hawkes, who was a publisher came to live at the house and in 1923 bought the freehold from Mrs. Neall. He was a director of the Amalgamated Press until his retirement in 1952 but retained an interest in publishing until his death in 1968. Among other magazines he published *Woman's Journal* and *Vogue* and in the social life of Welwyn ran a tennis club and in St. Mary's Hall he organised a badminton club.

Mr. Hawkes left the Mill House shortly before world war two and was succeeded by Geoffrey Elmer Garrett, from whom it was bought in 1942 by Imperial Chemical Industries Ltd. The Plastics Division headquarters were established at Welwyn Garden City at the outbreak of war and Mr. (now Sir) Peter Allen, the next resident of this historic old house was managing director of and later chairman of Plastics Division. He lived at the Mill House until 1952 when he moved to London on his appointment to the company's main board. Having received the honour of knighthood in 1957 for his services to export he served as chairman of ICI from 1968 to 1971. He travelled extensively abroad and among his other interests numbered the study of philately as well as of golf courses and railways. On the latter subjects as on his experiences in foreign lands he has published several books.

This charming old house was from 1952 to 1965 the residence of Dr. John Sisson who finally retired from ICI in 1970.

The grounds of Mill House apart from the part occupied by the mill pond formed part of the extensive rectory garden at the time of the celebrated Edward Young, our Poet rector of the mid 18th century. As well as three yew trees we can see four specimens of a tree that is not indigenous to Hertfordshire. This is the box which gives its name to Boxmoor in the west of Hertfordshire and to Boxhill in Surrey, which experts on the subject consider its native habitat. Because its wood is hard with a very fine grain, it used to be cultivated by wood engravers for their woodcuts, which formed a very pleasing feature of books printed in the 17th and 18th centuries.

The present owners of the Mill House are David Michael Cass, a marketing manager and his wife Berenice, who do all in their power to retain the charming old world appearance of what is one of Welwyn's most delightful houses.

So we must end what is we fear a very incomplete story of one of Welwyn's oldest houses.

Digswell Viaduct

A HERTFORDSHIRE ENGINEERING FEAT

SINCE the introduction of trains powered by diesel fuel, many of us look back with nostalgia to the trains of old, despite the vast quantities of smoke and steam that they used to belch forth. It was the dislike of these characters and the accompanying noise that motivated many landowners in the early days of railways. In these days people living in the vicinity of a projected airport are worried about the noise that would be created by increased aerial traffic. Most of us like a quiet life and it was this dread of noises and smoke that caused many landowners to register opposition when one of these new fangled railway companies said they would like to drive their 'iron horses' through their ancestral estates.

This type of opposition caused many railway companies to diverge from the more direct route they had originally planned.

In Hertfordshire the Great Northern Railway at first intended the extension of their line northwards from Hatfield to go through Kimpton, but Lord Dacre, whose seat was at Kimpton, or as sometimes called Whitwell Hoo, which was pulled down in 1957, objected on the grounds of its proximity to his grounds. As a consequence of this objection the GNR decided on a route further to the east which would pass through the future site of Welwyn Garden City, Welwyn, Knebworth and Stevenage on its way to Hitchin.

A direct result of this enforced change of plan was the construction of Digswell Viaduct, rightly ranked as an engineering wonder.

The chairman of the GNR, E. Denison and his board, employed a leading railway contractor of the day to build the viaduct. This was Thomas Brassey and the viaduct was designed by William Cubitt, the railway's chief engineer, on the

Digwell Viaduct. Gt Northern Railway

Hertfordshire Record Office

lines of a Roman aqueduct. Its vital statistics are: length, approx. 1,560 ft., height almost 100 ft. from road to railway track. It is carried over forty arches, each with a span of 30 ft.

Even today such an undertaking would be considered a great feat of engineering and in the forties of the last century, they lacked much of the knowledge and machinery that today would be considered absolutely essential for a work of this magnitude. When one surveys the viaduct it seems at first glance a colossal bridge to cross over tiny River Mimram, but the land on either side of the river consists of a wide valley in a deep bed of clay, which was saturated with water only 50 ft below the surface.

Thomas Brassey made his headquarters at the nearby Cowper Arms and employed upwards of 5,000 men, at a newly established brickworks in the vicinity. The greater part of his workers were a colony of Irish labourers known as navigators, soon contracted to 'navvies' also known as the 'Tray Bong Boys'. They were not slow in waking up the peaceful neighbourhood of Digswell and High Welwyn and every Friday night some of the workmen indulged in bare fist fights behind the Duck at Burnham Green. One of the bricklayers was the famous Tom Sayers, a doughty exponent of this primitive style of boxing. Some of them left their names inscribed on the viaduct, the first of which is George Nolan, so he may have been some kind of foreman or supervisor.

The 'navvies' lived in tarred and canvassed shacks, which must have been most unpleasant in bad weather, but it wasn't only labourers in those far off days who knew nothing of modern amenities.

The late Freda Davis, a member of an old Welwyn family, recounted that her grandfather George Davis employed a gang of men, who helped to carry the bricks. In order to obtain the clay for the 5,000,000 bricks required for the work, deep pits were dug in land about a quarter of a mile to the east of the viaduct. These pits were filled in and grassed over some years ago and are now marked by clumps of trees. They were dug in a field behind the site of the present Digswell Bury. This house was built about 1901 as a farmhouse and was occupied for several years by Mr. Lyle whose farm extended to the vicinity of the viaduct. It is now the residence of Mr. and Mrs. David Martin.

The work took about two years to complete and in one winter suffered several weeks' delay owing to frost. It was naturally unpopular with the stage coach drivers, who saw their occupation constantly eroded by the growing increase in railways throughout the length and breadth of the land. A story is told of one driver who would point to the growing structure of the viaduct and exclaim to his passengers: 'There, gentlemen, is my arch-enemy.'

The total cost of building the viaduct was about £64,000 and many times that amount would be needed in these inflationary times to carry out a comparable engineering feat.

It was opened for traffic in 1850 and on August 8 the first train crossed the viaduct. The passengers on the initial run consisted of the GNR directors and some senior railway officials and the first passenger train rain a few days later.

George Hudson, 'the railway king,' was among those who travelled in the first train. He apparently thought the task impossible and it must have conflicted with his own plans for railway development, because he is said to have spent a fortune in opposing the scheme, but when it was completed expressed his admiration for this latter-day wonder of Hertfordshire and indeed of the world.

Since those days of more than a century and a quarter ago it has been estimated that the Digswell Viaduct has carried a greater volume of traffic than any other bridge or viaduct in the world. It has of course required maintenance work at various times and in the later thirties was recased at a cost of £25,000.

Nearly 16 years later there took place one of the earliest railway accidents in England which indeed may have been the first in Hertfordshire. The tragedy took place not far from the viaduct in the tunnel north of Welwyn Station, as Welwyn North was called before the days of the Garden City, on the night of Sunday, June 10, 1866.

Three goods trains were involved and the incident began when a north bound train of empty coal wagons was forced to stop in the middle of the tunnel on account of a burst boiler tube. In those days the Midland Railway had running powers over certain sections of the Great Northern and a Midland goods train bound for Hitchin ran into the stationary coal train. To add to the confusion a meat train from Scotland ran into the wreckage of the two earlier trains. Its engine overturned and coal from its furnace ignited casks of oil carried by the Midland train and in all some hundred wrecked trucks comprised a terrible scene of devastation. A squad of 200 men was despatched to clear away the debris and the Hatfield fire engine was sent by the Marquess of Salisbury. The guard of one of the trains was severely injured and two men were killed. One of them was the guard of the coal train and a friend to whom he was apparently giving a free ride.

An inquest on the dead men was held at the Cowper Arms. At the official inquiry it transpired there was a misunderstanding between the signalman at Welwyn and his opposite number at Knebworth. The Welwyn signalman swore that he telegraphed to Knebworth to inquire whether the lines were clear and that he received the answer 'Yes', but the Knebworth signalman swore that he had said 'No'. And each man was positive that his story was right, no conclusion as to blame could be reached. However, it was pointed out that when the coal train came to a halt, the guard should have gone along the line to warn any train that might be following. One result of this calamity was an improvement in the system of signalling then in vogue.

William Ellis incognito

THE MIDDLE YEARS of the eighteenth century saw the publication of book after book by William Ellis, of Church Farm, Little Gaddesden; and in what is perhaps the best known of them, *The Country Housewife's Companion,* he acknowledged his authorship also of one called *The London and Country Brewer,* which had been published anonymously in three parts and a supplement.

Its title page proclaimed only that it was 'By a Person formerly concerned in a Public Brewhouse in London, but for Twenty Years past had resided in the

This four Wheel Drill Plow, with a Seed and a Manure Hopper, was first Invented in the Year 1745. and is now in Use with Wm. Ellis at Little Gaddesden near Hempstead in Hertfordshire. where any person may View the same. It is so light that a Man may Draw it, but Generally drawn by a pony or little Horse.

Kylin Archive

Country.' How long he was connected with the brewhouse was not stated, and this may have been deliberate in view of Ellis's disclosure in *The Country Housewife's Companion*: 'I was Executor to my Uncle's Will, a Brewer in London; which engaged me a little while in that Business.'

Although on the title page of *The London and Country Brewer* Ellis chose not to reveal that he was its author he laid enough clues in the text of it to give the game away. Local allusions begin on the very first page, with mention of 'those fine, pale and amber Malts made at Dunstable, Tring and Dagnal'; and later Pendley October beer comes in for special praise. Its fame, so Ellis averred, was 'well known not only throughout Hertfordshire but in several other remote Places, and truly not without desert, for in all my Travels I never met with any that excell'd it, for a clear amber Colour, a fine relish, and a light warm digestion.' He had 'had the Honour to drink' some at the house of 'the late Curious Simon Harcourt, Esq., of Penly,' whose customary invitation was 'You are welcome to a good Batch of my October.'

Probably Ellis had been one of those visitors to Pendley who had been regaled with 'a refreshment of this Cordial Malt Liquor . . . accompany'd with a good Breakfast or Dinner besides,' and it sounds as if he was writing from experience too when he added that many a richer man than Harcourt would think he was being generous if he gave 'a Yeoman his Neighbour, the mere Philosophical Treat of a look on the Spit, and a standing Drink at the Tap.'

Harcourt's 'October' was brewed by 'an old Days-man' who had been specially trained at his expense by a Welsh brewer, and as a result, according to Ellis, 'exceeded all others in these Parts afterwards in the Brewing of that which he called his October Beer.' In writing 'in these Parts' Ellis was giving away the fact that this was his neighbourhood and unwittingly affording a clue to his authorship of the book. But this was only one of many such clues. Divulging 'A Way to have Liquor little inferior to Claret, and yet pay but the Common Excise of Beer and Ale,' he stated that this was 'brewed by the late Dr. Brabbin . . . at his house at Berkhamstead, where it has often been preferred to Claret by his great Visitors, the first Sort of Gentry.' The wine was made with elderberries, but only 'the largest Sort,' their size being increased by a system of pruning. Dr. Brabbin had had one great advantage, Ellis alleged, for 'Berkhamstead St. Peters . . . may. justly claim the name of a most excellent Water for Brewing, and will make a Stronger Drink with the same quantity of Malt than any of the Well-waters.'

'Near, if not quite as good as Rain or River-waters' Ellis ranked pond water, provided 'there is a clean Bottom and the Water is undisturbed from the Tread of Cattle.' Indeed, pond waters were 'often prefer'd for brewing even beyond many of the soft Well-waters about them,' and he cited the case of 'a Maltster living within a few Miles of Dunstable, who was reputed to have the best October Beer by making use of his Horse-pond Black water.' Ellis's advice with 'muddy, greenish, or even an ill-scented Water' was to boil it. He himself had been 'often forced by Necessity to brew with such Water, having only a Current out of the common Road that feeds my Ditch, and that Pond in my Garden.' Another pond he commended was 'Blew-pot Pond on the high Green at Gaddesden in Hertfordshire,' the water from which, incidentally, was still being used for drinking in the nineteenth century.

In singling out Bluepot pond Ellis was coming so near home as practically to reveal his authorship; but elsewhere in the book he was bolder still. He seized the first opportunity of expressing his confidence that 'when Time has got the Ascendant of Prejudice, the whole Nation will come into the Practice of the invaluable Receipt publish'd in two Books, entitled, Chiltern and Vale Farming Explained, and, The Practical Farmer; both writ by William Ellis of Little Gaddesden near Hempstead in Hertfordshire.' This was 'a new Method how to steep Barley Seed in a certain cheap Liquor a Night and a Day, and then to lime and sow it.' He claimed, somewhat obscurely, that it was partly responsible for keeping down the price of malt, which was then 'about twenty Shillings per Quarter, and like to be so by the Blessing of God, and the Assistance of that invaluable excellent Liquor for steeping Seed Barley in, published in a Book entitled The Practical Farmer.' On another page he put in a good word once again for 'that incomparable and invaluable Receipt, for the Improvement of this Noble Grain, publish'd by William Ellis of Little Gaddesden near Hempstead in Hertfordshire'; and on yet another — just in case the point had been missed — he wrote 'Not only Brewers, but even Maltsters and Farmers in general are ignorant of this important Matter, nor when they would be sensible of it I know not, had not Mr. Ellis, a Farmer of Little Gaddesden near Hempstead in Hertfordshire, published the Secret in one of his Books of Husbandry.'

He could, using rather fewer words, have published the Secret in *The London and Country Brewer* itself. It cannot have been the fear of repeating himself that deterred him, for this he did continually; it can only have been his determination

Kylin Archive

to make his readers buy another of his books.

On the various methods of refining liquor he offered it as his impartial opinion that 'none, that I ever heard of, will answer like those most excellent Balls that Mr. Ellis of Little Gaddesden in Hertfordshire, has found out by his own Experience to be very great Refiners, Preservers and Relishers of Malt-liquors and Cyders.' These were for sale, and I suspect that it may have been only because there were no buyers that, in the last part of the book, he announced that he had 'at last been prevailed on, contrary to former Intentions, to publish the following Receipts of those most excellent Balls.' The long list of ingredients begins with powdered alabaster and oyster-shells; but there was really nothing special about these balls of his, for similar ones were in general use by brewers of his day.

If in spite of his claims Ellis had little new to impart he knew all the old tricks of the trade. Peter Kalm, the Swedish traveller who visited him and was not uncritical of his other activities, wrote that 'the Treatise he had written on Brewing is considered by several in England as the best of all his writings, because he relates therein his own experiences.' But was it entirely based on his own experiences? Although Ellis wrote 'I have always considered Experience as the only Touchstone of Truth' and claimed to have written about nothing that he could not personally vouch for, in fact Kalm recorded that he was often taken in by 'made-up stories his mischievous neighbours amused themselves by telling him.' It is hard to avoid the suspicion that one or two of his recipes came from this source and had been accepted by him untested. Certainly some of them have ingredients that do not make them sound appetizing: egg-ale. made of eggs and lean beef, and cock-ale, for which you 'boil the Cock in a Manner to a Jelly . . . and put the Liquor into the Cask . . .'

But these must not be dismissed out of hand, for meat was in fact often added to a brew to give it 'body'; and if Ellis's assurance that wild carrot seed, would 'make an Ale that will taste like Apricot Ale' takes some believing, the claims be made for his brews of elderberry will not seem far-fetched to anyone who has tasted that wine. In addition to the vintage that was considered superior to claret, he had a recipe for elderberry beer which made 'a most rich Drink, that they call Ebulum, and has been often preferr'd to Port-Wine.' Yet another elderberry wine, for which he gave the recipe in *The Timber Tree Improved*, 'has deceived a Gentleman I was in Company with, of great Judgment in many other Liquors; who took it for French Frontigniac.' This was made with white elderberries, which according to Ellis 'are generally bigger than the Red, and superior to them in Wine.' The white elder, from which this 'most noble Berry' was obtained, had been introduced into Hertfordshire, he wrote, in 1738, about thirty years before, 'by the late curious Simon Harcourt, Esq., of Penly, from whom I had many Cuttings that now grow in my Garden-hedge to a great Height.' They were then, he wrote, 'pretty common' and perhaps thereabouts they still are, for clusters of white elderberries were recently seen in a garden hedge near Ivinghoe common.

Readers of *The Timber Tree Improved* who wanted to obtain extra large elderberries, red or white, for their wine were referred by Ellis to 'the genuine Receipt' in 'my Supplement to the London and County Brewer.' Why then did he conceal his authorship of it when it was published? Probably it was because its fulsome praise of William Ellis and the repeated advertisements in it for his other books and his 'secrets' would carry more weight if they seemed to emanate from someone else.

Something had to be done to boost their sales, for these had fallen off disastrously when it was noised abroad that what he preached in his books he failed to practise on his farm, which visitors to it had reported to be in a sorry state. Whatever his failings as a farmer, and whatever misgivings one may have about him as a brewer, there is one field in which he cannot be faulted: as a salesman he was supreme.

Whitwell Hoo

SITUATED in one of the most charming and as yet unspoilt localities of Hertfordfordshire, which in this industrial age still retains its ancient rural character, there stood on a wooded plateau the old manor house known as Whitwell Hoo. From its upper storeys it was possible on a clear day to obtain an interesting variety of vistas of the surrounding countryside for many miles around. Students of local history will be aware that until shortly before the outbreak of the second world war Whitwell Hoo was the seat of the old Hertfordshire family of Brand, which played a great part in county affairs for several generations.

The county records prove conclusively that a manor house has stood on the site of the present building since the Middle Ages and was mentioned as early as 1287. Until the middle of the seventeenth century the manor was in the posscssion of the family of Hoo or de Hoo, who, like so many of our landed gentry, had their original home in Normandy. Susannah, the last heiress of this line, married Sir Jonathan Keate, baronet and alderman of London, who was Sheriff of Hertfordshire in 1665 and died in 1700. It was this lord of the manor who built the mansion, pulled down in 1956, and his initial 'K', together with 'I' and 'S' for Jonathan and Susannah, with the date 1661, can be seen just below the roof over the main entrance.

A memorial plaque to Sir Jonathan and Dame Susannah and several of their

*Overleaf/Whitwell Hoo House as it appeared in a lithograph in 1826/*F. Ballin.

descendants is affixed to the south wall of the church of St. Peter and St. Paul at Kimpton. Their grandson, Sir Henry Hoo Keate, sold the manor in 1732 to Margaret Brand, from whom it passed eventually to the then Lord Dacre, the holder of an ancient barony created in 1307. The twenty-third Lord Dacre was advanced a step in the peerage as Viscount Hampden in 1884, and it was the then head of the Brand family, twenty-fifth Baron Dacre and third Viscount Hampden, who was the last private occupant of the Hoo.

He was for several years Lord-Lieutenant of Hertfordshire and sold the property in 1938. Now vested in the Oxford University chest, the house was occupied as offices during the second world war by the London and North-Eastern Railway Company, and subsequently by Imperial Chemical Industries Limited, who relinquished their tenure in December 1954.

Etymologists will be interested to learn that there are two theories concerning the origin of the name of the house. By some authorities it is derived from the Anglo-Saxon word 'hob,' meaning a spur of land. The famous Plymouth Hoe is an example of this usage. Hence this term has often been applied to large houses standing on rising ground. The other theory, doubted by some historians, is that the name was borne by the forebears of the family of de Hoo before they left their ancient home in Normandy.

ICI always called the house Whitwell Hoo, but two noted local historians, the late Reginald Leslie Hine of Hitchin and the late William Branch Johnson of Welwyn, always referred to it as Kimpton Hoo. John Karrington, a farmer of Bramfield who died in 1810 wrote in his diary he had just gone to Kimpton Hoo. The boundary between Whitwell and Kimpton probably passed through the grounds. The house itself was in Whitwell, in the parish of St. Paul's Waldon and its telephone number was Whitwell 76; so this must be why ICI called it Whitwell Hoo. However, as the memorials to the Brand family are in the church of St. Peter and Paul at Kimpton, this would probably be the correct name of the Hoo.

For two years after ICI left the Hoo, the owners unsuccessfully tried to find a new tenant, but as their efforts were in vain, they reluctantly decided to have the property, with the exception of a few farm buildings, demolished towards the end of 1956.

In 1954, Frank Ballin wrote a farewell Elegy for ICI's final dance before their return to Welwyn Garden City.

This county landmark, has become just another memory of a bygone age.

FAREWELL TO THE HOO: AN ELEGY

Far from Black Fan's loud tempestuous strife,
    For many a year we've dwelt at Whitwell Hoo,
And led a calm secluded rural life,
    And hearken'd to the Friesians' bovine moo,

No more shall we in Welwyn's village street,
    Across the road from our time-honour'd church,
Where we each mourn our friends were wont to greet,
    Await the advent of the morning Birch.

Remember how across the snow-clad fields,
    To work we trudged on many a leaden day,
What time the National Coal Board's scanty yields,
    Made Summer Suns seem twice as far away.

In days now gone some spent their hours of ease,
    At bowls or on the verdant putting-green,
While others, whom more active pastimes please,
    Stroll'd to the lane, whence Kimpton's tower is seen.

No more shall we on Yuletide's festal eve,
    To Albert's gaily festooned bar repair,
And drink full deeply, ere we take our leave,
    And greet the comely lasses gather'd there.

But now must we these rural haunts forsake,
    And to the storied past say our farewell,
For change must ever mortal man o'ertake,
    And what Fate holds for us, no man can tell.

ENVOI

So ere we take our leave, kind Reader, hear,
    How we due care and meet attention gave,
The late lamented Thomas Gray, we fear,
    Who violently revolveth in his grave.

Lockley's
and the man who hated noise

George Edward Dering on a tight rope at Lockleys over the river Mimram Captain R. Neall MBE

LOCKLEYS, one of Welwyn's finest Queen Anne houses, is situated a short distance from the left bank of the little river Mimram, or Maran, on its way to Hertford, where it joins the Lea.

The present house was built in 1717 by Edward Searle, a successful London merchant, who like many businessmen sought to establish themselves as country gentlemen in estates not too far from the capital, where they still retained their business interests.

The name of the estate is thought to mean that it was originally the 'ley' or clearing of a Saxon called Locca. The greater part of the estate lies within the parish of Welwyn but includes a small strip in Datchworth.

The first mention of Lockleys in our county records tells us that in 1303 it was held by Agnes de Valence, the sister of Aylmer de Valence, to whom it came six years later on his sister's death.

The estate came to John Mogford of 'the manor of Lokkerbury.' This seems quite a logical name for Lockleys, as we find the name 'bury' applied to many large houses.

At about this time the overlordship of Lockleys, having passed through various heirs of Agnes, became vested in John of Gaunt, Shakespeare's 'time honour'd Lancaster' and thus formed part of the Duchy of Lancaster, held by the Crown since John of Gaunt's son ascended the throne as Henry IV.

In 1415 Lockleys was conveyed to Sir John Perient of Digswell, penonbearer and Squire of the Body to Henry IV and Henry V and was also Master of the Horse to Joan of Navarre, the second wife of Henry IV. Sir John and his son, also Sir John are commemorated in a well-preserved brass in St. John's Church at Digswell.

Thomas Perient died in 1545, when the manor was divided between his daughters Dorothy and Anne, whose husband Anthony Carleton, by his will founded a charity to help the poor of Welwyn. Anne gave 'a messuage and a rood of ground with the appurtenances, lying in Welwyn to the repair of the Church and to the relief of the poor of this Parish.'

The Church House, situated in this ground, was then converted into an almshouse and having later been in turn a workhouse, a police station, a post office and a private house, reverted to its original function in 1968.

At the time of the Civil War Edward Wingate, whose family came from Bedfordshire, in the words of the county historian Chauncy, 'made a fair warren to this seat, stocked it with a choice Breed of Rabbits, all silver-haired, and planted it with a great store of Walnut trees,' some of which, or their descendants, remain to this day.

It was Edward Wingate's son, Ralph, who sold Lockleys to Edward Searle, whose daughter Elizabeth married Charles Gardiner. In 1814 his son and namesake sold the manor to Sir George Shee, baronet of Dunsmore, Co. Galway, who was said to be descended from a second century King of Munster. A hundred and seven of his letters have been preserved, including some to the Duke of Kent, Queen Victoria's father.

He died in 1825 and was succeeded by his son, the second Sir George, who was appointed Minister Plenipotentiary and Envoy Extraordinary to the Court of Wurtemberg from 1832 to 1844. He died childless in 1870. He however never possessed Lockleys, as his father had left this estate to his widow Elizabeth Marie. She died in 1838 and left the manor to her daughter Letitia, who in 1839 married Robert Dering of Barham Court, Kent.

Their son was the gifted and eccentric George Edward Dering, who died in

January, 1911, a few days before his eightieth birthday. The story of his life and all his various activities would fill a fair-sized volume, but no history of the ancient manor of Lockleys would be complete without a short summary of his career.

He was a gifted engineer and a member of the Royal Society and also of the Iron and Steel Institute and Institution of Electrical Engineers.

At the age of twenty he exhibited some of his inventions at the Great Exhibition of 1851 and in the Hertford Museum can be seen the apparatus with which he constructed an electric telegraph line between Welwyn and Hatfield. He invented a new type of chair to hold the rails to the sleeper on railway tracks. At Lockleys he had a workshop and forge, where he employed some thirty men.

The accompanying photograph, kindly lent by his grandson Captain Richard Neall, shows Dering at the age of twenty-eight on the tightrope, when he used to cross the Mimram with Blondin, who was said to use this exercise as practice for his crossing of Niagara.

Everybody at Welwyn thought Dering was a bachelor and knew nothing of his marriage to Martha Dale in 1859 at Brighton where he was known as George Dale. She died in 1894 without knowing anything of his life at Welwyn. Dering returned to Welwyn in 1907 and spent the last four years of his life living in one room at Lockleys.

One of his peculiarities was an intense dislike of noise and he caused the Hertford road to be diverted from the neighbourhood of Lockleys to its present position at a cost of £20,000.

After his death numerous paintings and items of stationary were found stacked against the wall in the crates in which they had been delivered.

Lockleys then came to his daughter, Rosa Georgina, the wife of Arthur James Neall, an organist at Brighton.

Many Roman and pre-Roman remains were discovered when the new Hertford Road was being constructed and these Mrs. Neall presented to the British Museum.

In her lifetime she transferred Lockleys to her surviving son, Captain Neall, who sold the property to the Welwyn Garden City Company and now lives at Chichester.

This historic old house was bought in 1955 by Sherrardswood School, which celebrated its golden jubilee in 1968.

Hertfordshire's beacons

As Sir Henry Chauncy wrote in his *Historical Antiquities of Hertfordshire*, signals had been made 'many years in England in some places by lighting a Pile of Wood, heaped up together upon an Hill; in others by firing a Barrel of Pitch, fastened to the top of a Mast or a Pole in the highest Places of the County.' Then, in the time of Edward III, 'it was ordain'd that Standards with their Pitch-pans on the top of them, like the fashion of these Beacons, should be set up in every County.' The reason for this was that pitch gave a brighter and longer-lasting fire than wood. Even so its light would have shown up only at night, and because of this a stack of damp straw was also kept beside each beacon so that a column of smoke could be sent up in the daytime.

When the beacon was lit every man was to 'resort to his captain.' Thus 'by means of the beacons,' the German ambassador wrote home in 1545, 'the English say that they can anywhere muster 25,000 to 30,000 men in two hours.' Consequently, when invasion by Spain was feared in Elizabeth's time her Privy Council had only to issue letters to the Lords-Lieutenant (who had been appointed in 1557 to organize the militia of each county) ordering 'the Beacons to be made and sett up on all such places as hath been accustomed' and 'attended and watched.'

The Lord-Lieutenant of Hertfordshire who received these instructions was Sir John Cock, of Broxbourne; and he in turn issued a sheet of directions for the maintenace of the beacons under his charge. They were to be 'watched Daye and Night until Hallowtide be past' (for the watching was discontinued in winter, when invasion was not feared); and this was to be done 'by discrete Men onlie.' Each Lord-Lieutenant was under strict orders to see that no beacon was 'fired without apparent danger,' and to this end Sir John ordered that a straight stick was to be 'nayled upon the top of the Beacon having its point directlie towardes the other Beacon from which [it was] to receive the Warning whereby they shall be the lesse deceived upon the firing of anie other thing besides the Beacon.'

'By night some did always watch,' wrote Chauncy. 'and in old times Horses and Men, whom our ancestors call'd Hobelers, were plac'd at Posts in the daytime to give notice to the County of the approach of their Enemies.' These hoblers were light horsemen who rode 'hobbies' or nags. One was posted by each beacon and allowed beer money for watching the previous beacon in the chain. As soon as he saw it flare he was to light his own and then spur away to alert those members of the trained bands who could not have seen his signal.

Early in 1587 — the year in which Spain planned to launch the Armada — the Lord-Lieutenant of Hertfordshire received a further instruction requiring 'the beacons to be made ready and watched.' The watching must have been a tedious business, for it was not until Friday, July 19, 1588, that the commander of the English fleet at Plymouth learnt that the Armada had been sighted off the Lizard. Drake may have carried on with his game of bowls, but no time had been lost in firing the beacons. The Spaniards could see the lights of them leaping from headland to headland and knew that their fleet had been spotted. What they could not see was the chains of fires that ran inland across the country. There is no contemporary record of these, but Macaulay's rousing poem has in that:

'. . . on, and on, without a pause, until the bounded still,
All night from tower to tower they sprang: they sprang from hill to hill'

One of the towers and three of the hills were in Hertfordshire, for the county had three hill-top beacons — Amwell, Graveley and Therfield — and one on a church tower, or, as Norden put it in 1598, on 'the Steeple of St. Petere in S. Albans,' this being the highest point in the neighbourhood. Three more stood on the threshold of the county. One was at Pegsdon, on Deacon Hill, which perhaps is a corruption of Beacon Hill. Another was at Ivinghoe, although this is not shown on the maps of the time; its kettle and dismantled parts were kept in the church in the early eighteenth century. The third was the cresset beacon on Hadley church tower — though not the one that is there now, which dates only from the eighteenth century.

Kylin Archive

Hadley Church Tower and Beacon

It must have been Hadley beacon that started the chain across Hertfordshire, the last and most northerly link of which was at Therfield. Now from here Ely cathedral is visible on a clear day, so it may have been Therfield beacon that passed the alarm on to Ely, when:

'Broad and fierce the star came forth on Ely's stately fame,
And tower hamet rose rose in arms o'er all the boundless plain.'

The beacons did their work so well that by morning, according to Macaulay, even 'the burghers of Carlisle' knew that the Armada had been sighted. In the event, of course, it never invaded these shores. Its defeat was soon assured; and in the following year a note was sent to St. Peter's church with instructions 'to ring for our good success against the Spaniards.' 'Paid to ringers at that time,' the churchwardens' accounts record, '4s. 8d.' And so the church tower which the year before had blazed the alarm across the Hertfordshire countryside now pealed forth the news of England's victory.

For some years, however, further invasions were feared and instructions were issued that the beacons 'from tyme to tyme, be well repayred, and that everie thing be in a readiness for the necessarie use of them.' As late as 1596 a sum of nineteen shillings was paid 'for the watching of Therfield Beacon.'

None the less, as the fear of invasion died away some of the beacons were neglected. The one at St. Peter's church seems to have been the first in Hertfordshire to go. Although the churchwardens' accounts for the year 1605 refer to repairs to the bell tower, the upper bell loft and the steeple, and even include such details as 'nayling ye wethercock,' there is no mention of a beacon. Nor is there any sign of one on a large-scale plan of St. Albans dated 1634, which shows clearly enough the spire of St. Peter's church and the weather-cock. The last — and indeed the only — one of the county maps to show this beacon is Norden's of 1598; it does not appear on Speed's map of 1611, though the other three Hertfordshire beacons feature conspicuously.

This map was used in the civil war, in which Hertfordshire supported Parliament, and in this cause the beacons were brought into use again. Those which were strung along the Chiltern ridge — such as Ivinghoe, Pegsdon and Therfield — stood, as it were, on the rim of a saucer, looking out over the midland plain; and just as at the time of the Armada their position had enabled them to spread the alarm northward over this plain, so now in the summer of 1642 they stood ready to flash southward to London the news that the king had raised his standard in Nottingham, and after this they were watched anxiously for a signal of the approach of the Royalist army.

After the civil war was over, however, most of the beacons, having served their purpose, seem to have been allowed to fall into decay. At the end of the century Chauncy could only write that at Graveley 'a fair Beacon might lately have been seen' and at Therfield there 'lately stood a Beacon.'

About this time Therfield was described as situated 'among the Tops of small hills hanging over Royston,' and it was on one of these hills, to the west of the church, that the beacon had stood. From here, as Chauncy wrote, there was 'a fair and open Prospect towards the North over the County lying underneath.' As early as 1528 the hill had been called the Totehill, a name which signifies a look-out and which survives in the nearby Tuthill Manor.

The 'fair Beacon' at Graveley was also not far from the manor house, standing to the north of the village. From here it commanded a wide view and was admirably situated, in Chauncy's words, 'by a light burning Fire to give notice to all the Inhabitants round about, when any Enemies were coming.' So was Amwell beacon, standing as it did on the highest point of Hertford Heath, where it could be seen for miles to the east and to the west. The part of the heath on which it stood was then known as Beacon Heath, of which all that is left now is the green at Little Amwell.

This beacon lasted the longest of the four. It was found to be in need of repair in 1609 and again in 1622, 'to the great detriment of the whole republic,' so the inhabitants of the hundred were ordered to reapair it at their own cost as they had done 'from time immemorial' and two justices were appointed to see this done. By 1662, however, it had fallen down and Richard Goodman, a Hertford maltster, was accused of stealing the timber and ironwork. But that was not the end of it; four years later the justices were ordered to see that it was set up again.

This was no mean task, for these hilltop beacons were substantial structures, as the representations of them on contemporary maps suggest — even though the depiction of the hills on which they stood is exaggerated. Each consisted of a square wooden baulk sunk into the ground, with four diagonal supports at the foot and a circular 'kettle' on the top. This held the inflammable material and was reached by a ladder of cross-bars nailed to a spar leaned up against the baulk.

The materials needed to re-erect Amwell beacon at the end of the century comprised '170 feet of timber . . . great nailes . . . nails and coard . . . iron work . . . bricks and tiles-herds . . . a load of sand . . . lime . . . pullies and roapes . . . the kettle.' The timber had to be drawn from Butchery Green, a saw-pit made, and the finished product carried to the heath. Then there followed the business of setting up and 'underpinning the beacon.' In all 'the charge of the beacon erected on Hertford Heath' amounted to £35. 4s. 7d., which sum included the inevitable charge 'for beere and dinner at the framing and setting up of the beacon, 15s.'

For all this trouble and expense, within a decade — in 1702 — the beacon was described as 'very much out of repaire and ready to fall.' Someone was to be indicted for failing to repair it, but a helpless note in the margin of the quarter sessions book reads: 'Query, who to be indicted.' Evidently no scapegoat could be found, for the next spring the same marginal note is repeated. By then the beacon was 'ready to fall and likely to do mischeife,' and sure enough the next winter it was 'blowne down by the late Great Wind.' The chief constable was then ordered to 'take the timber, iron, and materialls of the said Beacon, and sell the same for the best price he can gett.'

So passed from the Hertfordshire scene the last of the county's beacons. Their usefulness had passed, but they had had their hour of glory when they blazed across the Hertfordshire countryside the news of the dreaded Armada.

'Such night in England ne'er had been, nor e'er again shall be.'

Hadley Church in 1837

Catchpenny Catnach

IN HERTFORDSHIRE'S newly acquired parish of South Mimms, on the corner where Wash Lane turns down from Dancers Hill Road, there is a hedge overgrown with brambles, interrupted by a green-painted gate. Behind it nothing is to be seen but tussocky grass and a few old fruit trees; of the building that was standing here a short while ago there is now no trace. This had been an inn called the White Lion back in the days when the road that ran past its door was not the byway that it is today but the highway from London to the north-west; it was in the early 19th century, when the new road in the valley below stole away the traffic, that it had to close.

As a house it had much to commend it — the accommodation of an inn and views of open country on all sides that can still be enjoyed from the site today — and an ideal country retreat to which to retire it must have appeared to the bachelor of forty-six who bought it in 1838. But when Jemmy Catnach 'of

An early woodcut of James Catnach Dover Publications

Monmouth Court, Monmouth Street, printer' became 'James Catnach of Dancers Hill, South Mimms, in the county of [then] Middlesex, gentleman' he was to find that the habits and associations of a quarter of a century were not as easy to throw off as he thought.

It was in 1813 that he had come down to London from Northumberland to take over his father's printing business. Catnach senior had gone bankrupt and left his son little more than an old wooden hand-press, some odd chipped type and a few worn wood-blocks, and with this material Jemmy set up the Catnach Press in Monmouth Court, Seven Dials. He began of necessity by improving with secondhand type and blocks, and he continued to do so even when he had built up a flourishing business. The same woodcut illustrated the funeral of every celebrity for years.

At auctions Catnach would buy up job lots of old printers' stock, some of the blocks dating from the sixteenth century, and these he would use regardless of subject. His verses on the death of Nelson were illustrated by the cut for 'A was an archer who shot a frog.' 'The dying child to its mother' by an angel appearing to an old man, and 'The heart that can feel for another' by a fierce lion.

These titles give an idea of some of Catnach's stock-in-trade. He was London's largest printer of halfpenny street ballads, sentimental and comic, while for only twice the price he offered 'strings of poetry' and 'songs, three yards a penny!' The words and subject mattered less than the tune, and Catnach is said to have kept a fiddle on his premises to test any new ballad offered him by having it sung: if he thought it would sell he paid its author half a crown. But he also printed and sold broadsheets (the newspapers of the poor), execution sheets, confessions and 'last sorrowful lamentation sheets.' The last were written, on behalf of the not always poetically inclined criminal, by the 'regular poets,' and the following is a typical specimen of their art:

I am condemmned all for to die
A death of scorn and horror,
In front of Horsemonger-lane Gaol,
At eight o'clock tomorrer.'

Dickens according to his biographer, 'thoroughly explored the ballad literature of *Seven Dials*,' and in one of the *Sketches by Boz* which he wrote in 1835 he described *Seven Dials* as 'the region of song and poetry — first effusions, and last dying speeches: hallowed by the names of Catnach and Pitts.' Pitts was Catnach's bitterest rival, and he had others; but his was by then the most famous name of them all.

Much of his fame and fortune he owed to the murderer John Thurtell. By having four presses working day and night for a week and running off 200 to 300 sheets an hour, he managed to produce 250,000 copies of 'The Full, True and Particular Account of the Murder of Mr. Weare by John Thurtell & his Companions, which took place on the 24th of October, 1823, in Gill's Hill-lane, near Elstree, in Hertfordshire.' For this his charge was 'Only One Penny,' and so popular did it prove that the hawkers who bought copies by the quire crowded out his shop and, to make room, he had to give them tickets to collect the sheets at his warehouse.

After the murder came the trial, and with it the prospect of more business for the Catnach Press, Jemmy Catnach brought in two more presses, employed more printers, and this time ran off 500,000 copies in eight days; but in his eagerness to get them out hot from the press he let many of his customers have copies for which he never received payment. Years afterwards a paper-worker told Henry Mayhew that the following recollected lines from 'The Life, Trial and Execution of John Thurtell' were 'quite in old Jemmy Catnach's style; for he used to write verses — anyhow he said he did, for I've heard him say so'; and this 'was just his favourite style':

'Come, all good Christians, praise the Lord,
And trust to him in hope,
God in his mercy Jack Thurtell sent
To hang from Hertford gallows rope.'

— and, it might be added, put £500 in Jemmy Catnach's pocket!

The thought that with Thurtell's execution this source of income had dried up was too much for him, and a fortnight later he issued a broadsheet headed 'We are alive again,' with the space between the first two words so artfully reduced as to look like 'Weare.' Many fell for this trick, but the word, 'catch-penny' was applied to it and this stuck for ever afterwards to the productions of the Catnach Press.

Illustrations from the Travels of Fortunatus

From 'The Saviour's Garland, a choice Collection of the most esteemed Carols'

There was not always a murder, a trial, an execution or a scandal to keep the presses turning, and in their otherwise idle moments they were used to turn out broad-sheets for the Christmas trade. These, which had religious themes, were twice the size of the ordinary broadsheets and were sold 'penny plain and twopence coloured,' which meant that blobs of colour were daubed on them by children. One of Catnach's Christmas broadsheets was called 'A Hertfordshire tragedy,' but we have not been able to trace its subject.

Printing also went on all the year round of cheap little books, called chap books, for children, and over these Catnach seems to have taken unusual trouble. In an age when most books written for children put their edification before their amusement, these chap-books were popular because they aimed first and foremost to amuse. Little, if anything, in Catnach's chap-books was original, but they did keep alive such traditional tales as 'Cinderella', The Children in the Wood' (as 'The Babes in the Wood' was called) and 'Jack the Giant-killer'. Others contained nursery rhymes, including 'Jack Spratt', 'The House that Jack Built', 'Cock Robin', 'Mother Goose', 'Simple Simon', 'Old Mother Hubbard' and some less familiar. But instruction was not entirely forgotten: 'a useful toy for little Miss and Master to learn their ABC' was the verse beginning 'A was for Archer', and 'The Tragical Death of an Apple-pie' was another.

Altogether there is no doubt that he justified his advertisement:

'JAMES CATNACH
to His
JUVENILE READERS

Little Boys and Girls will find
At Catnach's something to their mind;
From great variety may choose
What will instruct and amuse'.

It is more doubtful whether the next lines were justified by the crude little woodcuts that adorned his chap-books:

'The prettiest plates that you can find,
To please at once the eye and mind,
In all his little books appear,
In natural beauty shining clear.'

'Little books,' however, was a true enough description, for the smallest were no bigger than a pocket diary; these were the farthing boks that Catnach added to his stock of penny and halfpenny ones. And no quarrel can be made with the statements in his final couplet:

'He sells by Wholesale and Retail;
To suit all moral tastes can't fail.'

He mostly sold his wares to pedlars, who resold them at street corners or hawked them about the country to races and fairs. Since they sold them for coppers, it was in coppers that they paid Catnach and in coppers that every Saturday night he paid his employees, who would bring along their families to help them carry the load home. The remainder he would take in bags to the Bank of England, hiring a hackney coach for the purpose; but there were so many bad pennies among them that with these he paved the kitchen behind his printing office by embedding them in plaster of Paris. Even the good pennies people would not accept from him, fearing that they might be infected, until he boiled them in vinegar and potash so that they shone like newly minted coins.

Jemmy Catnach exemplified the maxim that if you take care of the pennies the pounds will take care of themselves, for by the time he retired he had made, if not the £10,000 he claimed, at least £5,000. But he soon found that the life of a country gentleman of leisure was not for him; he missed the activity and companionship he had known at Seven Dials. His business was still carried on there, and it was so that he could visit it from time to time, that he had chosen to retire to a spot not too far removed from it. His house was twelve miles away and only a quarter of a mile above the new Holyhead road, which had made travel to London easier and quicker.

As time went on he returned more and more often to his old haunts and stayed longer and longer, talking and drinking with his old colleagues. The gin which was their tipple he called 'stuff'; he himself drank whisky, not then a popular drink south of the border, but by ancestry he was a Scotsman, and proud of it. He claimed to be descended from 'Catnach, king of the Picts.' 'I am a Catnach,' he would boast. 'Yes, there's Catnach blood in me. Catnach — King Catnach.'

Perhaps it was his addiction to whisky that made him suffer with his liver, but he had become something of a hypochondriac and was always worrying now about his health. In January 1839 he made his will, and eighteen months later he wrote to his sister in London: July 4th, 1840. Dear Sister, — I have been very ill these last three weeks. I was obliged to send for Dr. Morris to cup me, which did some good for a few days; since then the pains have gone into my breast and ribs, and for the last three days I have kept my bed, and could take nothing but a little tea and water-gruel. I wish you to procure me 6 Bills to stick on my window-shutters, outside and in, 'This House to be Let,' and send them with ½lb. Tea as soon as possible.'

Under the July sun the currants were ripening in his garden. It was these he meant when he went on to write: 'I have had a great crop of black and red berries. If you choose I will send them up, and you can make some jelly for us both; let me know as soon as you can, say Wednesday morning, and I will make the Postwoman call for the parcel at Jackson's. I also wish you to enquire of Carr what is the lowest he will take for the rooms over Mrs. Morgan, by the ½ year. Yours truly, James Catnach. Pray send a paper of the execution of the Valet, and the trial of Oxford — Mrs. Westley has not sent me 1 paper since I was last in town, neither has Thornton.'

Between the lines of that postcript can be read his frustration at being cut off from all that was going on in London. No doubt he was happy to move into the rooms 'over Mrs. Morgan' in Monmouth Court, but his caution in taking them 'by the ½ year' was sadly justified, for early in 1841 he died of jaundice in his old shop. The house at Dancers Hill was still his, and his stone in Highgate cemetery reads: 'In memory of James Catnach, of Dancer's Hill, died 1st February, 1841, aged 49.' But his real memorials are those folk tales, fairy stories and nursery rhymes that, by his crude little chap-books, he helped to preserve for children of his day and of ours.

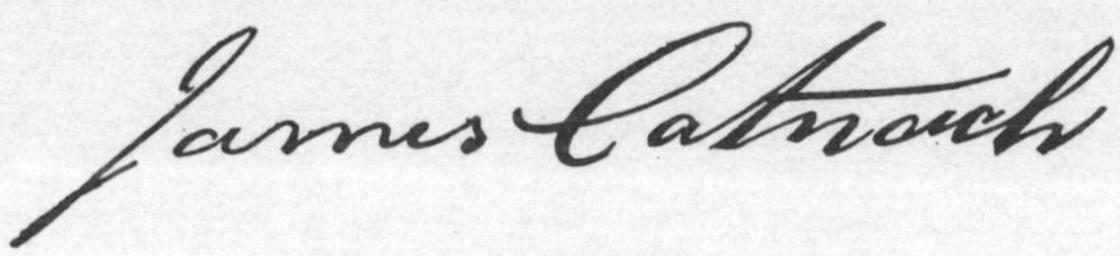

Jo Haynes

HIS FORTUNES AND FOLLIES

JO HAYNES, 17th century actor-extraordinaire, first came to the notice of the people of Hertfordshire as a quack doctor, selling a wonderful 'elixir' in the market place. Unfortunately, in Hertford he ended up in jail, 'accused of some indecencies.' Naturally, he was unwilling to show his face again in that town, but this in no way meant that the county had seen the last of him.

Audiences of country bumpkins held for him a fascination, acquired perhaps when he joined a company of 'strowling players' at Stourbridge Fair in Cambridge. This was the beginning of his dramatic career, which by 1668 had brought him to London. Here Pepys was among his audience. 'An understanding fellow,' was how the diarist described him the first time he saw 'one Hanes' dance: and two months later he had become 'the incomparable dancer of the King's house . . . a seeming civil man,' who also 'sings pretty well.' He had soon made his name as a comedian, and in the 1670s Dryden and Wycherley were writing parts for him.

One summer, when the London theatres were closed, he joined a company in Oxford, and it was there that, according to his biographer, 'not being contented with the Profits arising from Acting,' he 'found another way of getting Money, viz by Fortune-telling.' Though threatened with arrest and forced to return hastily to London, he had no intention of giving up so lucrative a pastime. He 'apply'd himself to base means to procure money,' according to *The Lives of the Gamesters*, in which incidentally there is also mention of 'a Richard Spaniard' called James de Domingo.

Did this rich Spaniard become a poor one by losses at the table? A James Domingo — was it the same person? — accompanied Jo Haynes, on August 1, 1676, to Ware. With them, too, was 'a woman in man's apparrell' called Sarah, who passed as Domingo's wife. They put up their bills and were soon doing a fairly brisk trade telling fortunes, three of which are preserved among the Quarter Sessions records. The first is clearly a young woman's and should surely have satisfied her: 'You shall be married Candlemas Day to a pretty tall merry-speaking man with black haire, a mole on his chin, you doe not know him yet his name is Simon Peters, a farmer's son, he is worth 80^{l} & heire to his father.' Another reads: 'I should advise you not to proceed in Law,' and a third — incomplete — runs: 'The water, has been an Enemy to you, and almost (spoiled your) fortune . . .'

For suchlike information John Hockley and John Gridley, both of Ware, paid 'sixpence a peice. James Domingo taking the money.' But on consideration they evidently felt they had been cheated and, since fortune-telling counted as fraud and was a punishable offence, decided to turn the two of them over to the law. They 'came into Ware togeather,' testified Hockley and Gridley, 'pretending to Tell ffortunes, both by publishing papers to that end, and also by doeing of it.'

Hence it came about that Haynes and Domingo, who had gone on to Bishops Stortford the next day to try their luck there, found themselves arrested. Haynes confessed that 'hee went out of London with a designe to assist James Domingo and naturall Magicke and other Artifices to tell fortunes,' and Domingo that he had been at Ware on the 1st of August, with his 'wife' and Haynes, and at Bishops Stortford on the 2nd. He admitted that 'the printed paper now shewed to him,' was his and that he 'did accordinglie practise the said Art of telling ffortunes.'

He and Haynes had also claimed, according to Peter Holdsworth of Ware, to 'give phisicke and cure almost all deseases by an Elixar as may appeare by their Bill.' If the bill brought the people in, Haynes knew how to talk them into buying his cure-all. 'Gentlemen,' he would say, 'I present you with my Universal Solutive, or Cathartic Elixir, which corrects all the cacochymic and cachexical Diseases of the Intestines: cure all internal and external Diseases, all vertiginous Vapours, Hydrocephalus . . .' and so on and so on. This may not have been the exact patter with which he cajoled the citizens of Ware, but it is a typical speech of his which happens to have been set down. In it he went on to offer his lucky hearers: 'My friendly Pill, call'd 'The never failing Heliogenes,' being the Tincture of the Sun, and deriving Vigour, Influence and Dominion, from the same Light; it causes all Complexions to laugh or smile, even in the very time of taking it; which it effects by dilating and expanding the gelastic Muscles . . .'

In this wise, no doubt, he blinded with science his audiences at Ware and Bishops Stortford, while Domingo raked in the money. Holdsworth alleged that they had said: 'Mony came in very Slowly at Ware by sixpence and 3 apiece, but at Bishop Stortford they gott 20^{l}.' Perhaps this was their mistake — to flaunt their takings. Although in his confession Haynes denied 'that hee tooke any mony, and p(re)tends whatever hee did was without any designe but as A ffrolicke,' according to Rivers Dickinson of Ware — whose testimony was supported by that of his fellow-townsmen. John Lawrence and Nathaniel Ford — 'Joseph Haynes as well as James Domingo did p(re)tend to tell ffortunes and take money and the said Joseph Haynes did boast theat hee had gotten ffive pounds and three Maydenheads at Ware and a broaken Shinne.' This, surely, was the comedian in Haynes playing for a laugh: a maidenhead was a coin of Queen Elizabeth's reign, but there can be little doubt that he had in mind a double entendre. As for Domingo, he admitted 'hee got aboat six and twentie Shillings' at Ware but claimed he 'got not above 7s. in Bishop Stortford.'

The punishment for a first offence of this sort was usually a whipping and confinement in the stocks, followed by an enforced return to one's last place of residence. Perhaps this is why a note is to be found in the Quarter Sessions records that Domingo 'hath noe houses but that his dwellinge and his wive's are at Doctor Revells in Salisburie Court, London.' Thither he was packed off, no doubt, accompanied by his 'wife' and Haynes — nursing his broken shin.

If Joe Haynes' reception in Hertfordshire proved to be a cool one, he contrived to captivate his London audiences. He is also said to have set up a booth in Bartholomew Fair and, in 1685, to have produced there a droll called *The Whore of Babylon, the Devil and the Pope.* Then in 1692, 'after so many Years treading the Stage, where both in my acting and capering Days (to my Vanity be it spoken) I made no inconsiderable Figure,' he turned to play-writing. This was despite 'these elderly Years upon my back' — he was forty-five! — and was due to the same causes that had sent him into Hertfordshire — 'A dull World, want of Business and much Idleness, with not overstockt a Pocket.' As to how his tragedy. *A Fatal Mistake, or the Plot Spoil'd,* would be received, 'now hang me, he declared, 'as great a Fortune-Teller as I have been' — was he thinking of that excursion to Ware? — 'all my Prognostics failed to reveal.' Presumably it turned out to be little to the taste of the town, for he published no more plays.

Epilogues and prologues, however, he continued to write and, frequently, to speak One he delivered in the guise of a madman and another, in 1697, in the habit of a cavalry officer and mounted on an ass. Although eventually there came a time when 'age and infirmities had rendered him incapable of those exalted performances he was formerly master of,' in between money-making jaunts in this country and abroad he was to be seen on the stage almost to the end of his life. But at last, after 'taking to his bed for some time,' in 1701 Jo Haynes died, aged fifty-three, in Hart Street, Long Acre. He was buried in the churchyard of St. Paul's Covent Garden, and before the year was out there had appeared two biographies of him.

His life, according to one of them, had been 'all of a piece, the Comedian both on and off the Stage'; off-stage 'his Disguises had more of the Humourist than the Imposter,' for 'His Frauds were rather to be call'd his Frolicks.' This was the very term Jo himself had used when denying that he went to Ware for gain; but to those citizens of that town who laid out their sixpences — whether they handed them to him or to his accomplice, James Domingo — his frolics must have seemed rather like frauds!

Manor of Mardleybury

THE ANCIENT and attractive manor of Mardleybury, at Woolmer Green, derives its name from an Anglo-Saxon word meaning 'the weasels' clearing' and gave its name to a pre-conquest owner, Alward de Mardeley.

Edith of the Swan-neck, the wife of Harold II, was the feudal overlord and it is interesting to note that in the entry relating to this manor in Domesday Book she is referred to as queen. The Normans, of course, regarded Harold as a usurper and, in their records, accord him no higher title than that of count.

After the conquest, the manor came into the possession of Robert Gernon, a Norman follower of King William. As in several other instances, the former Saxon owner was allowed to remain as the vassal of the Norman overlord, for we find that Alward de Mardeley is mentioned as one of Domesday inquisitors for the hundred of Broadwater. We hear no more of this family until 1288, when the lord of the manor was Philip de Mardeley, probably a descendant of Alward. Philip had a daughter called Pagana, but she apparently did not succeed him, as it was held soon after by Adam de Twynham, who died in 1307.

An unfortunate holder of the manor was Bartholomew de Badlesmere in the time of Edward II. In his earlier years he was one of the king's most strenuous supporters and served in Parliament for several years, but later joined the rebel barons under Thomas, Earl of Lancaster. The rebel forces were defeated at Boroughbridge in 1322, and Bartholomew, having been taken prisoner, was sent to Canterbury, where he was executed for treason and his estates were forfeited to the Crown. His son, Giles, who was fourteen years of age at his father's death, found favour in the eyes of Edward III and was restored to his father's favour and estates. He, however, only enjoyed his heritage for some four years, as he died

F. Ballin

Mardleybury, a manor house in Welwyn Parish

young in 1338. His wife was Elizabeth, daughter of William Montacute, Earl of Salisbury, by whom he had no issue, so at his death his estates fell into abeyance between his four sisters, of whom Margaret, the wife of Sir John Tiptoft, eventually inherited Mardleybury.

In the reign of Henry VIII the lady of the manor was Gertrude, daughter of William Blount, Lord Mountjoy, and wife of Henry Courtney, Marquess of Exeter. This marquess was one of the numerous victims of Henry's displeasure in his declining years and, like so many of the nobility in those stormy times, suffered on the scaffold in 1540. As Mardleybury was not sequestered on his attainder, it must be presumed that Gertrude held the manor in her own right.

She was herself attainted in the following year and the estates, having thus come into the hands of the king, were granted in 1546 to Sir Nicholas Throckmorton, one of the stewards of the queen's household. Sir Nicholas sold the manor in 1555 to Thomas Nicholls, a mercer of London, who held it for only a year. The next owner was John Foster, and we learn that in 1598 Sir William Lytton of Knebworth purchased certain lands belonging to 'Mardelye burye.'

Sir William shortly afterwards granted a mortgage on the manor to Henry Spencer, and we know definitely that it was this same Lytton who was lord of the manor in 1617. His family had been in possession of the adjacent manor of Knebworth since the time of Henry VIII, and among later holders of this famous name we call to mind the first Baron Lytton, the illustrious novelist of early Victorian days, and his son, the first Earl of Lytton, who ended a distinguished pro-consular career as Viceroy of India.

The manor of Mardleybury was thus a possession of the Lyttons for well over three centuries until Lady Hermione Cobbold, the elder daughter of the second earl and wife of Mr. Cameron Cobbold, the then Governor of the Bank of England, disposed of the property in 1950.

As is the case with so many old houses, there have been tales from time to time of ghosts and poltergeists and as our northern neighbours say 'things that go bang in the nicht'. There is certainly a hidden chamber which may have been a priest's hole in the days of the widespread persecution of members of the ancient unreformed faith.

We have not been able to trace any records of any Catholic family who lived here, but as the Lyttons never seemed to have lived here and it was let for a long period as a working manor, if any of our readers should know of any Catholic connection the house may have had, it would add to our short account of its history.

Neither Mr and Mrs Hudson, who lived there in the early seventies and showed a deep interest in the history of their home, nor Nigel and Valerie Durrant, to whom they sold the house early in 1980 have experienced any personal manifestations of the supernatural.

Mardleybury is among the oldest and most historically interesting houses in Hertfordshire and we hope may long remain free from modern developments which have in so many cases detracted from much of our heritage from the days of long ago.

Thomas Kitchin, Engraver of St. Albans

'THOMAS KITCHIN Senior of the Borough of Saint Albans in the County of Hartford Engraver' — thus did the hydrographer to George III describe himself in the will he made in November 1780.

Although he was living in St. Albans at that time his working life had been spent in London, where from about 1738 he had a shop at the Star in Holborn Hill. Here he sold book-plates and portraits, but his stock-in-trade consisted mainly of maps, and among them were several of Hertfordshire.

His earliest, which appeared in May 1748 in the *London Magazine,* was a small map measuring 8½in. by 6½in.., and the next — published in the following year in collaboration with Thomas Jefferys — was even smaller. It was about 4½in. square, and since the county was not the right shape to fit into this area there was nothing for it but to compress it from east to west! Beneath this very distorted Hertfordshire were listed details of the fairs, markets and parliamentary representation of the towns in the county.

In May of the same year — 1749 — John Hinton, a bookseller of St. Paul's Churchyard who had previously employed Kitchin to engrave maps for him, engaged his services on a more ambitious project than heretofore. His intention was to issue a detailed map, on large imperial paper, of one county every month until the whole country had been covered. Hertfordshire's turn came early, for in August 1749 the *London Evening Post* contained an advertisement: 'This day is publish'd (price only one shilling) a new Improv'd map of Hartfordshire, from the best surveys & intelligence . . . by Thomas Kitchin, geographer. Being the fourth of a set of the county maps now publishing monthly.'

Kitchin defended his spelling of 'Hartfordshire,' as opposed to the form

Hertfordshire that was gaining currency, on the grounds that several earlier authorities had favoured that form and that 'the Armorial Bearing is a Hart in the Water, of which Hartingfordbury is plainly a Compound. These reasons [he was satisfied] are clear enough to confirm the true spelling of Hartford.'

The claim in the advertisement that the map had been compiled 'from the best surveys & intelligence' did not mean that the county had been surveyed afresh but that advantage had been taken of the most up-to-date existing maps — in particular one by John Warburton. As in his map, the main roads — though not the minor ones — were shown, and on these the 'true Measured Distances between Town and Town' were recorded down to the nearest furlong. This was a useful convention that went back to Ogilby's road map of 1675, which also introduced the distinction — against adopted by Kitchin — between roads that were hedged or fenced and those that were 'Open and Healthy.' The latter, which ran unfenced across unenclosed country, were represented by broken lines; such were the tracks across Royston Downs between Barkway and Royston and around the village picturesquely described as 'Barley or Bergley among the Hills.'

The scale of the map was a little over half an inch to the mile — large enough to show considerable detail and to leave room for notes here and there. Thus a note to the west of Wheathampstead recorded 'These parts produce plenty of excellent wheat,' and another by the side of Watling Street 'This Roman Way continues to Holyhead and St. Davids in Wales.'

Celebrities of the past were not forgotton: Abbots Langley was 'famous for the Birth of Pope Adrian IV,' Offley (by tradition) for the death of Offa. But more consistently the 'Nobility and Gentry' of Kitchin's own day were noted against their 'Parks and Seats' — in order, no doubt, to induce them to buy copies of the map. Hyde Hall near Sawbridgeworth, the seat of 'Jocelyn Bt,' Kitchin noted had been 'in this Family ever since 1249' — a span of 500 years.

Hertford, being the county town, was singled out for special treatment in the form of a description, historical and topographical, in the margin of the map. From this those who purchased a copy learned that 'The situation is healthy and pleasant, and the people deal largely in Wheat, Malt & Wool.' Hitchin —' reputed the second Town in the County for number of Houses, Streets and Inhabitants' — had to be content with a somewhat cramped description in the body of the map, recording the fact that 'It was formerly of great note for the

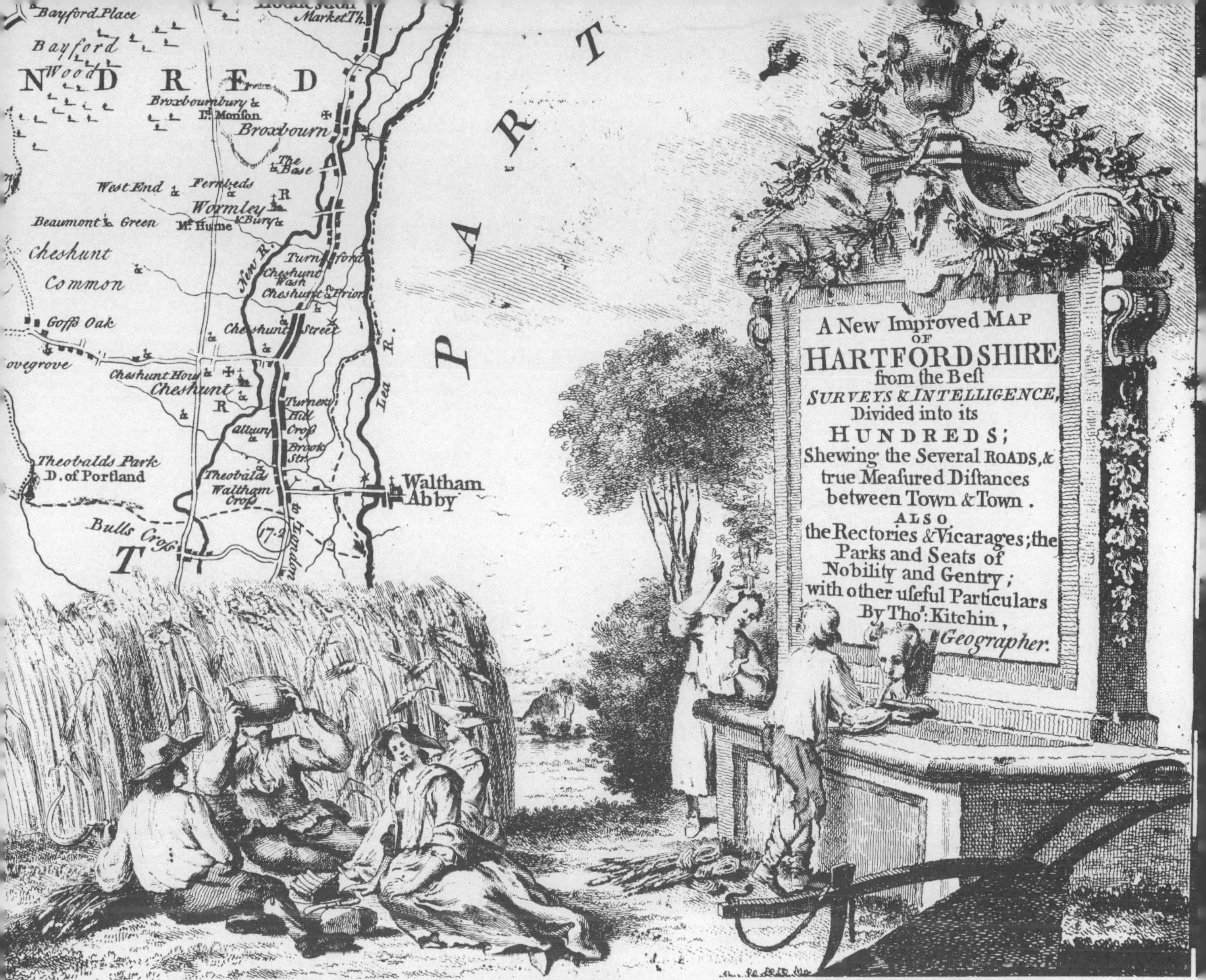

A detailed vignette by Thomas Kitchin, geographer of a rustic harvest scene *Hertfordshire Record Office*

Woollen Manufacture but now that Trade is quite lost; however, the Market for Grain, especially Malt, is still much frequented.'

So as not to overcrowd his map with words, however, Kitchin used an almost bewildering array of conventional signs to provide a mass of useful information. The result was that a place of the importance of St. Albans fairly bristled with symbols, indicating that it was a post-stage and parliamentary borough and that it had rectories, vicarages, charity schools, religious houses, a watermill and — nearby — a windmill.

There was no symbol for spas, for though 'Barnet Wells' and the 'Medicinal Waters' at Northaw were still noteworthy enough to be mentioned on the map their heyday was past. Of St. Osyth's well 'on the E. side of the River' at Bishop's Stortford, Kitchin wrote that its 'Water was held in great Esteem,' implying that this was no longer so. Some villages, too, had formerly been relatively more important: Flamstead had been 'once a Market Town'; so had Ashwell — and had a corporation to boot.

Altogether it was a map full of information, both practical and antiquarian, with the added attraction of a vignette depicting a rustic harvest scene. In a half-cut field of corn rested one reaper with a sickle and another taking a swig from a harvest barrel, while two country wenches laid out a meal and a third talked to a swain drawing water from a fountain. Two plaited corn dollies and a plough — symbolic of Hertfordshire's fame as a wheat-growing county — completed the picture.

As well as being sold separately from 1749 the map was reprinted in 1760 in 'The Large English Atlas' which Kitchin published in collaboration with Emmanuel Bowen; and in 1763 he produced another, though much smaller, map of Hertfordshire for *England Illustrated*.

His partner Bowen, who had in his last years been almost blind, died in 1767. But Kitchin had a son, to whom he had given the Christian names Thomas (after himself) and Bowen (after his partner), and when Thomas Bowen Kitchin was old enough to join his father in the business it became known as Kitchin and Son.

In 1769 Kitchin produced yet another map of Hertfordshire — even smaller than the last and once again much distorted. None of these later maps is to be compared with his large-scale map of the county, which continued to have a steady sale.

By 1776 the business had evidently been sold to 'W. Hawkes (Successor to T. Kitchin) 59 Holborn Hill' and perhaps this is when Thomas Kitchin senior retired to St. Albans. But some of the stock-in-trade of his shop must have remained his, for he bequeathed to his son the 'Copper plates, prints, fixtures and so forth in my late Dwelling House in Holborn and which he received at his marriage' in addition to a legacy of £50. To his wife, Jane, he left £750 as well as the household goods, furniture, plate, pictures, wearing apparel 'and every other article . . . now in my possession at my house in Saint Albans.'

It was there in June 1784 — four years after making his will — that Thomas Kitchin died, the *Gentleman's Magazine* including a brief obituary of the 'Hydrographer to his Majesty.' But his name lived after him, for though the contents of his shop were sold up after his death copies of his large map of Hertfordshire continued to be printed. They were being advertised for sale as late as 1824, though in the following year the plates — by then well worn — were sold as old copper for a shilling a pound.

Despite the fact that copies had thus been printed over a period of threequarters of a century they are now by no means common.

First man to fly in England

WHERE will the balloon land? was one of the competitions at 'Expo North Mymms,' held at Welham Green in September 1970; and this was no ordinary balloon but 'a giant hot air balloon' with a basket appended for pilot and passengers. Unfortunately its ascent was very brief, lack of wind and slight damage preventing it from being released to drift across country as had been intended. The occasion had been planned — to quote the programme — 'to commemorate the first-ever aerial voyage in England and landing of Vincenzo Lunardi at North Mymms on September 15, 1784,' and the field chosen for its launching was very near the spot marked by the 'balloon stone' where — reputedly — Lunardi landed. But was it, in fact, there that he came down? Where *did* the balloon land?

The story of his flight across Hertfordshire has been told more than once. It began just after two in the afternoon from the Artillery Ground in London, whence the balloon drifted north-westward over Highgate and seemed to be heading towards St. Albans, then veered to the north and passed over Barnet. Looking down on the countryside spread out below him, Lunardi was entranced; 'The face of the country had a mild and permanent verdure . . . the rivers meandering . . . the immense district beneath me spotted with cities, towns, villages and houses, pouring out their inhabitants to hail my appearance.'

But these details were lost to sight as he rose higher: now 'the earth . . . appeared a boundless plain, whose surface had variegated shades,' from which, however (so he claimed), he could still distinguish, when four miles up, the cornfields from the pasture lands. He claimed also that the motion was so steady that 'I drank, eat and wrote just as in my study,' and to prove this point he wrote a

Hertfordshire Record Office

long screed which he cast overboard, addressed 'To any person or persons who may pick up this letter.' It was found, he was later told, by Mr. Casamajor, of Potterells, 'not very far from the milestone on Northaw common, while out a-shooting.'

The balloon itself was seen 'hovering over Northaw common,' for Lunardi, having been up now over an hour and feeling the effects of the cold, had decided it was time to come down. At half past three he contrived to bring his balloon 'within three hundred yards of the earth, and moving horizontally, spoke through my trumpet to some country people, from whom I heard a confused noise in reply.' The voices he heard were those of twelve men and thirteen women — among them William Harper, of Hatfield, and Thomas Blackwell, Thomas Moore, John Richardson, Mary Crawley, Sarah Day and Mary Butterfield, all of North Mymms — who were mowing and raking oats in a field in that parish. Here it was that the balloon came down, though it rested on the ground long enough only for Lunardi to disembark a kitten he had had aboard, which was nearly dead with cold.

It was Horace Walpole's opinion that Lunardi 'had full right to venture his own neck, but none to risk the poor cat,' which according to the *Morning Post* had to be destroyed. Yet Lunardi later exhibited 'the two little Animals, a cat and a dog, which shared with him the Dangers of that hazardous and uncommon Voyage.' He certainly knew how to draw the susceptible English public; and one stifles an ungenerous suspicion that it was not the identical cat!

It had been picked up by Mary Butterfield, said to have been only nine years old, who made a quick bargain by selling it to a gentleman who rode up on horseback. This was probably Nathaniel Whitbread, a farmer of Swanley Bar, who declared on oath that 'the machine . . . did not actually touch the ground more than half a minute,' for though he called on Harper and his colleagues to hold it Lunardi told them to keep clear when they tried to do so. Promising to 'gratify them by ascending directly in their View,' he threw out some sandballast, and the balloon — its grapple dragging up some loose oats as it skimmed across the field — rose into the air. From about twenty yards up Lunardi, through his trumpet, shouted 'that he should soon be out of sight,' though in point of fact he 'continued in sight at a very great height for near an hour afterwards.'

He soon took up his pen again, but (he wrote later) 'my ascension was so rapid that before I had written half a page, the barometer had fallen to 29 degrees.' Having fastened his letter 'with a corkscrew to my handkerchief,' he dispatched it to the winds and, ultimately, to the Hertfordshire countryside below. His 'plates, knives and forks, the little sand that remained, and an empty bottle' followed in quick succession; if there was anyone to witness their arrival it must have seemed unaccountable!

Whether they were found or not, all except one of his, 'dispatches from the clouds' (as he called the letters that he dropped) were picked up and 'preserved, as our people [the Italians] would relicks of the most celebrated saints.' As he dropped his last letter, 'fixed to a leathern belt,' he watched it 'on its passage, for several minutes.' Below it the countryside still looked 'like an extensive plain, with the same variegated surface.'

Where was he now? The balloon had been kept in sight by an observer in a post-chaise as far as Hoddesdon, and at Bramfield John Carrington of Bacon's Farm 'saw him plane as he came over Bacons, he was at a Great Hight for his Boloon was 30 feet round but apeard no biger than a Boys Kite.' Carrington recorded that he 'took his course East over Codicot, Wellwin, Tewin, Bengeo & Landed him selfe in a Little Meadow at Standon Green End, he throwd his line out & was pulled Down by a young woman in the meadow, who was fritned at first and Run away, thought it the Devell, till he made her sensable and gave her 5 guineas.'

This was sixteen-year-old Elizabeth Brett, and the story of how she came to Lunardi's assistance, 'George Phillips saying he was too short and John Mills saying that he did not like it,' has been told before in *Hertfordshire Countryside*. The balloon was taken to a Mr. Hollingworth's house at Thundridgebury and Lunardi to the Bull inn at Ware, where he was introduced to William Baker, the Member of Parliament for Hertford.

Baker not only entertained Lunardi at his home, Bayfordbury, but undertook to mark each of the places where he had come down to earth by means of a stone 'with a suitable inscription.' At Standon Green End — in the words of John Carrington — 'Baker had a great pipble stone which had lane in Bengeo street . . . remoovd to the place he fell & a Brass plate put theiron with the Account.' The plate was designed to 'let posterity know, and knowing be astonished, that . . . Vincent Lunardi . . . in this spot revisited the earth . . .' It astonished posterity for nearly a century before it was replaced by a replica in 1875, engraved — as presumably the original was — with a drawing of the balloon.

There is no doubt that this stone marks the correct spot, for William Baker stated that the balloon came down in a meadow called Long Mead, and this was the name given on the tithe map to the field where the stone stands. But can the same be said of the 'balloon stone' that stands at the corner of Huggins Lane, Welham Green, in North Mymms parish? This was not of Baker's erection but was put up little over a decade ago at a point already known as Balloon Corner but not — as far as I have been able to discover — previously marked in any way.

The 'balloon stone' is engraved with these words: 'Near this spot at 3.30 in the afternoon of September 15th, 1784, Vincenzo Lunardi, the Italian balloonist, made his first landing whilst on his pioneer flight in the English atmosphere. Having handed out a cat and a dog, the partners of his flight from London, he reascended and continued north-eastward.'

In actual fact, only the cat was handed out; the dog stayed aboard and 'performed the journey with the greatest calmness and resolution' according to one account, though, 'almost spent' at the end of it according to the *Morning Post*. But the stone may be incorrect in a more basic way, for it seems to me that it is in the wrong place!

Baker lost no time in establishing exactly where Lunardi had landed and 'ascertained the place with sufficient precision' by interrogating, among others, Nathaniel Whitbread, William Harper and Mary Butterfield — 'the very girl who picked up the cat' — and by inspecting the marks where the grapple had dragged the ground. It lay (he wrote) 'about half a mile to the eastward of the sixteen-mile stone, on the road leading from London to Hatfield.' This was the Great North Road, and the milestone can be placed, from a Sixteen Milestone Field on the tithe map of 1839, at the point where Shepherds Way leaves that road. Baker also described the field as 'adjoining to the road leading from the said turnpike road to the northward on the left' — a somewhat confusing description which seems to mean that the field adjoined, on the left, a road which went north from the Great North Road. The only road east of this which it could be is Kentish Lane, which then left the Great North Road at the same point as Shepherds Way.

Possibly the stretch of country southeast of Kentish Lane was at this stage still one large field, for it was — as Baker wrote — 'part of the lately inclosed common of North Mimms.' He stated that it lay 'in the manor of the Duke of Leeds' and described it as 'a large ploughed field belonging to John Hunter, Esq., of Gubbins.' The enclosure award was dated April 1782, and one of the two parcels of land allotted to John Hunter lay in the corner of the parish north of Shepherds Way; but in June of the same year he acquired the land that adjoined it on the east and extended as far as the parish boundary, which had originally been allotted to the Duke of Leeds.

Baker recorded that, on the enclosure of the common, when it was cleared a great bonfire of roots and rubbish burnt for several days in the field where two years later Lunardi was to land. Because of this, 'the common people having heard of a burning mountain in Italy,' they called the field Italy or Etna. Since Lunardi was in the employ of the Neapolitan ambassador in London, the coincidence of his landing in a field so called could not fail to strike Baker, who wrote to him: 'You hardly conceived, when you dropped, that you was so near anything that had connexion with Naples.'

Now if we turn again to the tithe map compiled half a century later we find five fields in this area called First, Second, Third, Fourth and Back Hitneys — a name that looks very like a corruption of either Italy of Etna, or a combination of the two. The reason for the name had no doubt been forgotten by then, and Hitneys was what it sounded like. The initial H is easily explained, for this letter was very frequently added to place-names that began with a vowel. Presumably the large field called Italy or Etna had been gradually split up — on a map of 1805 it is shown as partly subdivided — into the various Hitneys that appear on the tithe map.

But which of these contains the spot where Lunardi landed? The deposition of William Harper stated that he 'perceived a large Machine hovering in the air,

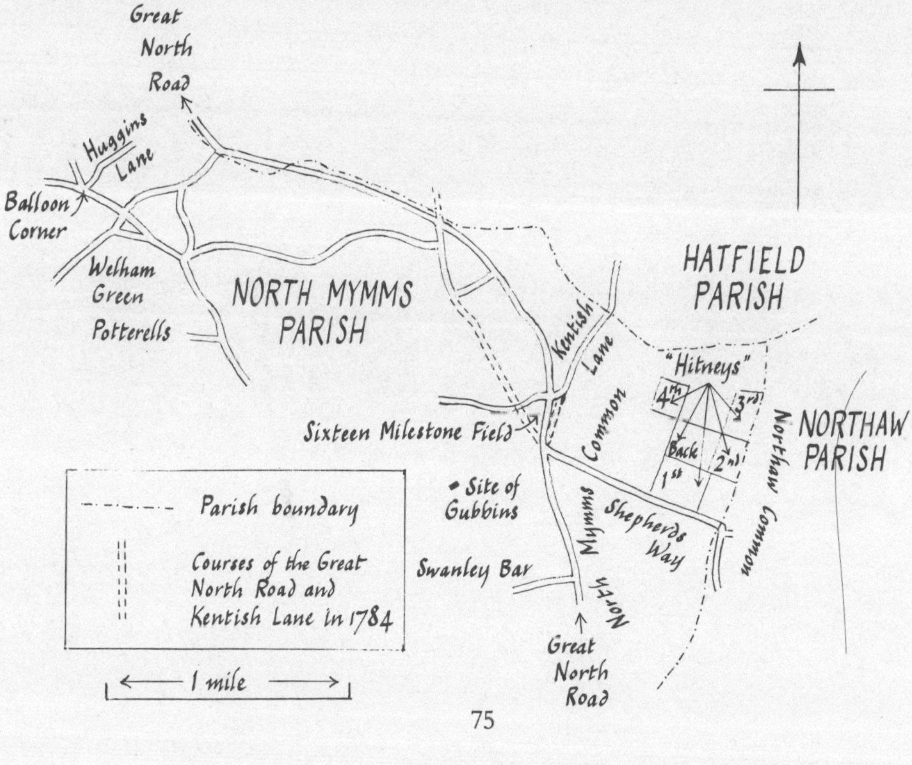

and gradually approaching the ground, near the boundary line of the Manors of Northaw and North Mimms'; and Baker wrote: 'The particular spot in the field is on the east side, very near the boundary line between the manors of Northaw and North Mimms.' It is the fields called Second and Third Hitneys that lie on the parish boundary, still marked by a half-submerged boundary stone.

They are the only fields that tally with every detail in Baker's description; the 'balloon stone,' on the other hand, stands at a spot that allies with none. True, the name of Balloon Corner was in existence 100 years ago; but however far back the tradition may go that this was where Lunardi touched down the accounts written at the time seem to make it quite clear that it was not here but nearly three miles away.

Three days after the landing Baker stated that 'a common hedge-stake only marks the spot'; what became of his intention 'with . . . the permission of Mr. Hunter . . . to erect a stone there' is a mystery. Perhaps his confidence in that gentleman's co-operation was misplaced and the sight of his ravaged field of oats left Mr. Hunter unimpressed by Lunardi's first landing on English soil.

Kylin Archive

Panshanger and the Cowpers

About two miles west of Hertford, in a well-wooded estate through which runs the little River Mimram, there stood until recent years one of the most extensive private houses in Hertfordshire. It was built in the early part of the nineteenth century and consisted of a long stucco building of two storeys and attics, ornamented with battlements and angle turrets in the Gothic style of that period. It had a central tower of three storeys that projected slightly from the main building and overlooked the park and the river, which was at this point artificially enlarged into a small lake.

There is no mention of Panshanger in Domesday Book, in which there is a record that Geoffrey Runeville held one hide in Blakemere of Geoffrey De Bech, and it is conjectured that Panshanger was carved out of Blakemere after the conquest. The first mention of the name is in a record of 1198, in which it is called Pansangra. According to one authority, the first syllable is the name of an early owner, and 'hangra' is thought to mean 'a wooden slope.' It was an ecclesiastical possession in the Middle Ages, like so many other estates, and belonged to the prior and convent of St. Bartholomew in Smithfield. In the fourteenth century the estate was successively held by Agnes de Valence, John Darcy le Cosyn and William de Melkescope, who also possessed the right of freewarren in Digswell, Datchworth and Ludwick. An inquisition taken at Hertford in 1446 confirmed Walter Chivell as lord of the manor of Panshanger and Blakemere.

In the time of Henry VIII, like the manor of Mardleybury at Woolmer Green, it formed part of the possessions of Gertrude, Marchioness of Exeter. After her attainder it reverted to the Crown, which soon afterwards granted it to Nicholas Throckmorton. It was later purchased by a member of the family of

Slaney, and it was formerly thought that this was Sir Stephen Slaney, sometime Lord Mayor of London in the reign of Elizabeth I. Later researches have, however, proved that this supposition was erroneous. The male line of the Slaneys failed in the early part of the eighteenth century, and the son-in-law of the last of that name sold the manor in about 1720 to the Right Honourable William Cowper, who soon afterwards built a mansion at Cole Green.

Sir William Cowper, Baronet, the father of the William Cowper who purchased Panshanger, was one of the commissioners appointed to treat with the Scots in 1706 regarding the proposed union of the parliaments, and in the following year was appointed Lord Chancellor by Queen Anne, who created him Baron Cowper of Wingham in Kent. He resigned with Godolphin and the other Whig ministers in 1710, but was again made Lord Chancellor after the accession of George I, who in 1718 created him Viscount Fordwich and Earl Cowper. During his second chancellorship he acted as Lord High Steward at the trial of the Scots lords in 1716 and also at the trial of Robert Harley, Earl of Oxford, for treason. Among his other activities he voted against the South Sea scheme and was a successful opposer of a bill 'for the more effectual suppression of blasphemy and profaneness,' by which all person who denied the doctrine of the Trinity or the inspiration of the Holy Scriptures were subjected to certain penalties, and those preachers who denied the fundamental articles of the Christian religion were deprived of the benefit of the Toleration Act.

The wife of this famous chancellor was Mary Clavering, and in her capacity as Lady of the Bedchamber to Caroline of Anspach, when she was Princess of Wales, had detailed knowledge of much of the secret history of the period, which she recorded in a voluminous diary, covering the period from 1710 to 1714. After Cowper — for the second time — resigned from the office of Lord Chancellor in 1722, he was suspected of being a secret Jacobite supporter. In order to save her husband from being compromised Lady Cowper destroyed some of her papers, which are reputed to have contained material concerning matters relating to high politics, as well as various court intrigues and scandals.

The former chancellor died in 1723 at Cole Green in the house recently built by his son, who then succeeded him as the second Earl Cowper. The second earl was a Lord of the Bedchamber from 1733 to 1747 and was also Lord-Lieutenant and *Custos Rotolorum* for Hertfordshire and a member of the Royal Society. He died at Cole Green in 1764.

Hertfordshire Record Office

Panshanger House from an old engraving

His son, George Nassau Clavering, was during his father's lifetime M.P. for Hertford from 1759 to 1761, but after succeeding to the family titles and estates as third Earl Cowper, he spent most of his later years in Italy and eventually died at Florence in 1790. Through the influence of the Grand Duke Leopold of Tuscany he was created a Prince of the Holy Roman Empire by the emperor Joseph II in 1785. He was a famous connoisseur of painting and amassed a great number of the 200 pictures which later were one of the chief glories of Panshanger until the house was demolished. The collection included paintings by Rembrandt, Van Dyck and Titian, as well as family portraits by Sir Joshua Reynolds, Sir Thomas Lawrence, Sir Peter Lely and Sir Godfrey Kneller, and is listed in his *Treasure of Art in Great Britain* by Dr. Waagen, who visited Panshanger in 1835 and 1856.

George Nassau was succeeded in turn by his eldest son, George Augustus Clavering, the fourth earl, who died unmarried in 1799, and by his second son, Peter Leopold Lewis Francis, the fifth earl. The latter is noteworthy in the history of his family and in the annals of Hertfordshire for the fact that he pulled down the house at Cole Green in 1801 and erected the noble residence at Panshanger, which was, however, not finally completed until some twenty years later in the reign of George IV. By his marriage in 1805 to Emily Lamb, daughter of Peniston Lamb, first Viscount Melbourne, he became brother-in-law to the statesman who was later to become the young Queen Victoria's favourite Prime Minister. He died in 1837, and some two years later his widow married the mercurial Lord Palmerston and was thus sister to one Prime Minister and wife to another.

The noted eighteenth century poet William Cowper (1731–1800), whose 'cups, that cheer, but not inebriate' must have formed a welcome text for the Victorian 'blue-ribbon' brigade was a near relation of the Earl Cowper.

The next owner of Panshanger was his son, George Augustus Frederick, the sixth earl, during whose lifetime there occurred a very serious fire which very nearly destroyed the house. In 1856 he was succeeded by his son, Francis Thomas de Grey, seventh and last Earl Cowper, who was sent by royal command to Denmark in 1865 to act as envoy extraordinary for the investiture of King Christian IX with the Order of the Garter. This monarch, as readers of Tennyson will recall, was the 'sea-king,' whose beautiful daughter, Alexandra, had recently married our future King Edward VII. The seventh earl was Lord-Lieutenant of Ireland from 1880 to 1882, and at his death in 1905 the earldom of Cowper with its subsidiary titles became extinct.

The last Countess Cowper continued to live at Panshanger until her death in 1913, when the house and estate were inherited by her niece, Lady Desborough, a famous beauty of the Edwardian era. One of her sons was the talented poet Julian Grenfell, a member of that numerous company of his generation who met an untimely death in the first world war. An earlier literary member of the family was the eighteenth-century poet William Cowper, a great-nephew of Lord Chancellor Cowper, who is remembered for his translations from the classics as well as his verse.

Mention must be made of the Panshanger Oak of great but uncertain age, which is accounted one of the most famous trees in Britain. Many years ago it was struck by lightning and is now but a shadow of its foremost self.

With the death of Lady Desborough in May 1952 the history of Panshanger as a private house came to an end, and by order of her executors it was pulled down towards the end of the following year. So ended another chapter in the story of Hertfordshire manors that are no more.

The Right Honorable William Cowper, Lord High Chancellor of Great Britain
Hertfordshire Record Office

WILLIAM SHAKESPEARE.

Theatrical Scenes

'THE POET'S pen . . . gives to airy nothing a local habitation and a name.' So wrote Shakespeare, who gave one of his own airy nothings a local habitation in Hertfordshire. This was the imaginary scene in *Richard II* which he placed in the Duke of York's garden at King's Langley, where the gardener 'set a bank of rue . . . in the remembrance of a weeping queen.'

In *Henry VI,* however, history or legend had set the scene for him. The interlude in St. Albans where the imposter Saunder Simpcox claims to have had his sight restored at St. Alban's shrine, was taken by Shakespeare from a story in Grafton's chronicle, though he elaborated on it by making Simpcox claim also to be a cripple. The threat of a whipping was enough to make him find his legs again, which the gullible townsmen of St. Albans acclaimed as a miracle.

The battles of St. Albans and Barnet, which occur in the same play, Shakespeare again based freely on the historically not very reliable chronicles available to him. When he wrote that the Duke of Somerset met his death, in fulfilment of a prophecy,

'Underneath an alehouse' paltry sign,
The Castle in Saint Albans.'

he was repeating a tradition that appeared in the chronicles of Grafton, Hall and Holinshed.

From Holinshed, too, Shakespeare's contemporary William Rowley took the story of St. Alban and wove it into his play *A Shoemaker a Gentleman.* One scene of this is set near Verulam, where Amphiabel and Albon are captured. The Roman emperor swears 'I will drag them hence in chains to Holmhurst Hill, three miles from Verulam,' and the play closes with this vow:

'A church the, and a beauteous monastery
On Holmhurst Hill, where Alban lost his head,
Offa shall build; which I'll St. Albans name,
In honour of our first English martyr's fame.'

The play *St John Oldcastle* perpetuates another St. Albans tradition — that the fugitive Oldcastle escaped capture there. It has scenes set in two St. Albans inns — the Bell and the Shears — and of these the Bell is located with such exactness as to suggest that it was a reality: 'Here's a few straggling houses beyond the bridge, and a little inn where carriers use to lodge.' St. Michael's village answers this description, and it is known that there was an inn called the Bell there at that time — in all likelihood the same building that is now called the Six Bells.

Oldcastle himself was not the only real person to be made, in the play, the subject of fictional episodes, Sir Richard Lee of St. Albans has a son who is murdered; Lee mistakenly accuses Oldcastle of the deed, and his trial in Hertford is the final scene of the play.

The sober fact is that Lee had no son; nor did Robert Fitzwalter, at one time warden of Hertford castle, have the daughter named Matilda whom tradition ascribed to him and whom Robert Davenport made the heroine of his play *King John and Matilda*. This has scenes in Hertford castle and Barnet, in both of which places the king captures Matilda only to have his prize snatched away from him again.

Several contemporary playwrights, however, wrote plays that drew on no traditions, but were simply romances which they gave realistic Hertfordshire settings. Naturally they chose those parts of the county best known to them — the towns on the roads out of London. Thus Thomas Heywood made Barnet the scene of part of his play *The English Traveller.* Here is the description of the town which he put into the mouth of one of its characters:

This Barnet is a place of great resort
And commonly, upon the market days,
Here all the country gentlemen appoint

A friendly meeting; some about affairs
Of consequence and profit — bargain, sale,
And to confer with chapmen; some for pleasure
To match their horses, wager on their dogs,
Or try their hawks some to no other end
But only meet good company, discourse,
Dine, drink, and spend their money.'

It has sometimes been stated that Thomas Heywood — as Well as John Heywood, an earlier playwright lived at North Mymms. If it is true, he would have known Barnet well; but did he? He failed to mention that it was at this date first and foremost a meat market; nor does he seem to have realized that it was then in Hertfordshire, for he made a character who finds another in a tavern there say 'Oh, sir, are the needle, and if the whole county of Middlesex had been turned into a bottle of hay I had been enjoined to have found you out.'

When Ben Jonson wanted a setting for his play *The New Inn* he too chose Barnet, that town of many taverns. At 'the Light Heart in Barnet' takes place the whole action of the play, though it must be admitted that he added a little local colour to show that he had a real acquaintance with the town. There is a reference to the 'footman's inn at the town's end, the stocks,' but then every town and village had its stocks.

Barnet lay on both the Great North Road and the Holyhead road, which ran through St. Albans. The first of these was not as busy then as it was later to be; but 'the way between St. Albans and London' was quoted by Shakespeare, who may have travelled along it on his way to and from Stratford, as an example of something familiar to all.

John Fletcher in his play *Wit without Money* referred to a jounrey along this stretch of road, mentioning in particular St. Albans and 'Mims'; and James Shirley in *The Witty Fair One* wrote of a character holding out her hand 'as the post at St. Albans that points the way to London.' This is something he would often have seen, for he had been a schoolmaster in St. Albans before he followed that same post to London to become a playwright. Among his plays was one called *The Tragedy of St. Albans*, but this has unfortunately been lost.

For a scene actually set on this road we must turn to William Bullein's

Dialogue against the Fever Pestilence, which, while not written for the stage, is set out in play form. It consists of the imagined conversation of a party leaving London to escape the plague in the middle of the sixteenth century. Reaching Barnet, one of its members says 'We will not tarry now, because every inn is pestered with Londoners and carriers. . . How like you this town, dame?' His wife replies 'A pretty street; but methink the people go very plain; it is no city as I do suppose by their manners. What house is this at the town's end, compassed with a moat?' 'This is called the Fold,' comes the answer, 'and here before is Dancer's Hill and Ridge Hill.' 'What great smoke is in yonder wood?' asks his wife. 'God grant it be well.' 'It is nothing,' her husband reassures her, 'but making of charcoal in that place.'

The wood was presumably Hadley Wood; and when he continues 'How like you this heath? he must have been looking across Gladsmuir Heath, for he goes on to recount how the battle of Barnet took place there. This was then almost within living memory; and one of the party recalls that his grandfather was there 'when the battle was pitched and appointed to be foughten near unto this windmill.'

After 1603 there was less traffic on the Holyhead road, according to the chamberlain of a Ware inn in Thomas Dekker's play *Northward Ho!* This chamberlain had previously been at an inn in Dunstable, and, when asked why he left it, replies 'Faith, sir, the town drooped ever since the peace in Ireland. Your captains were wont to take their leaves of their . . . wenches . . . at Dunstable, but your only road now, sir, is York.' By this he meant the Old North Road to that city, which ran through Ware.

'Wife,' says one character in the play, 'on with your riding suit, and cry 'Northward Ho!' . . . Let my prentice get up before thee, and man thee to Ware, lodge in the inn I told thee of, spur, cut and away!'

The play in fact both opens and closes at an inn in that town, called by the same character 'dirty Ware' and described by another as 'a town where hosts will be familiar, and tapsters saucy, and chamberlains worse than thieves' intelligencers.' That is to say, they provided the highwaymen with information about the baggage and proposed routes of travellers staying at their inns.

Could there be in the vow that one character makes — 'I will be as true to thee as Ware and Wadesmill are one to another' — an implication that the two towns were in league in this way?

Beyond Ware, Dekker also mentioned 'Puckeridge five mile further,' though it was perhaps unrealistic to make one of his characters say, 'Tis a quarter of an hour's riding.' He also referred to Royston; and he showed his acquaintance with the Old North Road nearer London in his play *The Witch of Edmonton.* Though set in that town and its neighbourhood, this has several references to 'Chessum,' which was one contemporary spelling of Cheshunt.

Two others — 'Chesson' and 'Cheston' — occur in another play, *The Merry Devil of Edmonton.* In this a father, to prevent his daughter from marrying the man of her choice, sends her to 'Cheston nunnery,' which stood near Turnford. But he reckons without her rescuers, one of whom cries 'Blood, if all Hertfordshire were at our heels, we'll carry her away in spite of them.' In this they have the assistance of the Merry Devil, who swears that if need be:

'I'll make the brinish sea to rise at Ware,
And drown the marshes unto Stratford bridge;
I'll drive the deer from Waltham in their walks
And scatter them like sheep in every field.'

These were the deer of Waltham Forest in Essex, which it was a crime to kill; but this does not deter the host of the George inn at Waltham Cross, in the play, from planning a poaching expedition and declaring 'I'll fence with all the justices in Hertfordshire, I'll have a buck till I die.' There are scenes set in the forest, the nunnery and the George. Perhaps this was a real inn, for a speech by a character in a play called *The Parson's Wedding* — 'I cannot amble nor ride like St. George at Waltham' — suggests the existence of one with a signboard depicting the saint on horseback.

Two more Waltham Cross inns feature in Francis Beaumont's play *The Knight of the Burning Pestle*. One is 'the Red roaring Lion,' which may have been the inn now called the Britannia, for this was originally the Red Lion; the other is the Bell, which according to the play stood 'at Waltham town's end.'

When the knight — an English Don Quixote — arrives here under the illusion that it is an ancient castle offering knights hospitality the host plays a trick on him. Imitating his own high-flown phraseology, he tells him that 'at the north end of this distressed town' there dwells 'an ugly giant' called Barbarossa. This is in reality one Nick the barber, and the scene shifts to his shop, where Nick allows himself to be vanquished and his customers — all parties to the hoax — to be released.

Puckeridge gets another mention in this play, and the way Waltham was then pronounced is revealed by the following ingenious piece of rhyming:

'Good Mistress Luce, however I in fault am
For your lame horse, you're welcome unto Waltham.'

So much for the plays of Shakespeare's time. There is space for only the briefest mention of two later ones — Charles Macklin's *Man of the World*, which takes place near Hadley, and *The Importance of Being Earnest*, the setting of most of which is the imaginary 'Manor House, Woolton, Hertfordshire' — for the time has come to bring down the curtain on these Hertfordshire scenes.

Gulliver's travels through Hertfordshire

The Holyhead Road in Hertfordshire, as depicted on an 18th Century road map

WHEN THE CENTENARY of the birth of Jonathan Swift was celebrated, a special exhibition was staged at Moor Park, where for a time he lived. This, however, was not the Moor Park in Hertfordshire, but the one in Surrey that was named after it. Swift never lived in our county, yet there was a cross-section of it that he knew well, and a part that he mentioned in *Gulliver's Travels*.

The mention occurs in chapter two of the second book, in which Gulliver finds himself in the land of the giants, Brobdingnag. He describes how he is taken in a box 'to show me as a sight upon a market-day in the next town, which was put half an hour's riding, about two and twenty miles from our house.'

The preposterous idea — as it must then have seemed — that such a distance could be covered in a mere half-hour was, of course, intended to illustrate the different scale of things in Brobdingnag. But what is interesting is that Gulliver later says 'Our journey was somewhat farther than from London to St. Albans.' This is very accurate, for St. Albans, then reached circuitously by way of Kitt's End, Dancer's Hill, Mimms Wash, South Mimms, Ridge Hill and London Colney, according to Ogilby's contemporary map of the Holyhead road, was exactly twenty-two miles from London.

Thus Gulliver, before his voyage to Brobdingnag, must be supposed to have travelled this stretch of road; and in this respect Gulliver is Swift himself. He took it almost every time he travelled either between London and Ireland, where he lived most of his life, or between London and Leicester, where his mother lived. From 1689, when he settled at Moor Park, until her death he seldom let a year go by without visiting her at least once, taking a coach or hiring a horse on the rare occasions when he could afford it and travelling in a wagon or on foot when he could not.

Coach travel was, however, something he disliked. Of a coach journey along this same road from Aldersgate to Chester he wrote:

'Soon, by ev'ry hillock, rut and stone,
Into each other's face by turns we're thrown.'

It must, in fact, have been very like Gulliver's journey in his box, in which he 'was terribly shaken and discomposed.' It may not be too fanciful to suggest that the notion of travelling in a box which was 'close on every side, with a little door for me to go in and out' recalled to Swift his uncomfortable journey in the Chester coach; and this might account for his fixing on the comparison of the distance Gulliver travelled in the box with that from London to St. Albans. This coach journey Swift detested so much that he ended his verse on it:

'Next time I do protest, Sir,
I'd walk to Dublin 'ere I'd ride to Chester.'

Impossible as this is, there is a reference in *Swiftiana* to 'his journeys on foot from Dublin to London'! More realistically, it is recorded elsewhere that though he 'often went in a waggon' he 'more frequently walked from Holyhead to Leicester, London, or any other part.' It was on foot, for instance, that he went in May 1694 to Leicester on his way to be ordained in Ireland.

Although his living was an Irish one, he found occasion most years to visit London. On one such journey he carried in his pocket the manuscript of *A Tale of a Tub*, the book that was to stand in the way of his preferment in the Church; and the journey he made in December 1707 was another that was destined to be a fateful one. From Ireland he went to Leicester to see his mother and then broke his journey from there to London at Dunstable.

This was the last stage on the Holyhead road for travellers to London, so it is not surprising that at his inn he met a party travelling there by coach from Ireland. It consisted of a Mrs. Vanhomrigh, widow of a Lord Mayor of Dublin, and her family. It was to this chance meeting that Swift must have been referring when he wrote three years later of the elder daughter, Esther, that he:

'Had met her in a public place
Without distinguishing her face.'

Kylin Archive

Above a rare wood engraving of Jonathan Swift by Grandville, below, 'A mighty concourse of people appeared upon my arrival, full of wonder at the sight of so prodigious a vessel', Gulivers Travels.

Kylin Archive

Mrs. Vanhomrigh, on reaching London, wrote 'We have had a very successful journey here without the least accident.' But she was overlooking one accident, slight in itself, that was to have lasting consequences.

At the inn Esther had spilt some coffee, and this seems to have been what attracted Swift's attention to her, for in a letter to her twelve years later he suggested compiling a history of their friendship 'from the beginning . . . an exact chronicle of twelve years from the time of spilling of coffee.'

Having made the family's acquaintance in this way he renewed it in London, where he was soon seeing so much of them that Esther — known as Hessy, from which he coined the name Vanessa — fell desperately in love with him.

He left on horseback in May 1709 to see, for the last time, his mother in Leicester. His memorandum book records that he travelled about thirty miles a day and that his route lay through St. Albans and Dunstable. Returning from Ireland in the following year, he took five days to get from Chester to London and described himself as 'weary the first, almost dead the second, tolerable the third, and well enough the rest.' Late in life he claimed: 'I . . . can, or at least could, ride five hundred miles on a trotting horse,' and wrote that he rode after health 'like a post-boy.'

He had always had this obsession with exercise for the sake of his health. When, in June 1713, he had to return to Ireland to be installed as dean of St. Patrick's in Dublin he toyed with the idea of walking all the way to Chester, accompanied by one man and covering ten miles a day. 'It will do my health a great deal of good,' he noted in his journal, 'and I shall do it in fourteen days.' As he would have to walk 182 miles it is as well that he abandoned this idea on being given a horse! The night before his departure he spent at the home of his printer, John Barber, and there, before retiring, he dashed off a letter to the lovelorn Vanessa he was leaving behind: 'I hope this journey will restore my health; I will ride but a little every day; and I will write a common letter to you all, from some of my stages; but directed to you.'

He did not quite keep to his promise. On the following morning, June 1, Barber rode with him as far as St. Albans, where Swift gave him a letter to take back, addressed to Vanessa; but from Dunstable, where he slept his first night after riding thirty-four miles, he addressed his letter to her sister Moll. A sharp rebuke came from Vanessa by return: 'Sr. Now you are good beyond expression in sending me that d[ea]r voluntary from St. Albans. . . Pray why did not you remember me at Dunstable as well as Moll? . . . You have not kept your promise of rideing but a little every day. 30 miles I take to be a very great journey.'

He did not mend matters by writing from Chester not to her but to her mother: 'I writt to Hessy by Barber from St. Albans. . . . I could not see any marks in the chimn[ey] at Dunstable of the coffee Hessy spilt there; and I had no diamond ring about me to write any of your names in the windows.' This letter Vanessa took 'very ill,' asking 'Have you once thought of me since you wrote to my mother at Chester?' The answer — though it was never sent — was that he was thinking now of that other Esther who awaited him in Ireland — Esther Johnson, to whom he gave the name of Stella. To her he wrote from Chester: 'I am come here after six days . . . a noble rider,' but he confessed that he was 'terrible weary.'

He must have been more weary still later that year when he posted back to London on hired horses that cost him £2/10/-. From Coventry, on September 8, he rode sixty-two miles before stopping for the night at 'Market Street' in Hertfordshire, which was of course the village we know as Markyate. 'Full of good inns' as this was according to Ogilby, it is not unlikely that Swift stayed at the one that has survived from his time — the Sun. This inn catered for pack-horse traffic, and it is known that 'he generally chose to dine with wagoners, hostlers, and persons of that rank; and he used to lie at night in houses where he found written over the door "Lodgings for a Penny" ' — though he used to pay a few extra pence for clean sheets! It was not only to save expense that he chose to stay in these places and to travel sometimes in carriers' carts, but out of 'his desire of surveying human life through all its varieties,' as Dr. Johnson put it. Swift himself wrote that never did he see so much of the life that is worth seeing as in his earlier travellings to and from Leicester.

But these visits were over, for his mother was dead. In 1714 he returned to Ireland, and this time Vanessa followed him, unbidden, with her sister. Both had died there before Swift travelled back to London in March 1726 — not through Hertfordshire this time but by way of Oxford. In his baggage was the manuscript of *Gulliver's Travels* and, having arranged for its publication, in the August he took the coach back. 'I felt,' he wrote, 'the extreme heat of the weather, the inns, the roads, the confinement and closeness of the uneasy coach, and wish'd a hundred times I had . . . a horse.' But he was pleased when he reached Ireland in a week, having expected to be there 'with moderate fortune in ten or eleven days.' He wrote to Pope: 'What a quick change I made in seven days from London to the Deanery, through many nations and languages unknown to the civilized world. And I have often reflected in how few hours, with a swift horse or a strong gale, a man may come among a people as unknown to him as the Antipodes.' Perhaps it was this reflection that had given him the idea of *Gulliver's Travels*, in which he made a gale wreck his hero on the island of Lilliput and on Brobdingnag.

A year later a gale stranded Swift himself on an inhospitable coast. He had returned to London, but soon learnt that Stella lay ill in Ireland; and on September 18 he set off in the coach to Chester. This was as far as it went, so he posted on horseback to Holyhead; but though he was there within a week of leaving London he had to wait as long again before a boat could take him across to Ireland, the first one he set out in being driven back by a storm. When at last he reached Stella she had only three months to live. After her death he never mentioned her name again, though he himself lived on for another seventeen years. Nor did he ever come back along the road to London, but stayed at the deanery, becoming more and more of a recluse until, at the end, his mind gave way.

In the rectory at Welwyn Dr. Edward Young, the author of *Night Thoughts*, must have recalled an occasion some thirty years before near Dublin when he had seen Swift 'gazing upward at a noble elm, which in its uppermost branches was much withered and decayed.' 'I shall be like that tree,' Swift had prophesied; 'I shall die at the top.'

Kylin Archive

Dr Rosalind King

Wymondley Hall, a beautiful Elizabethan house reputed to have been built about 1593

The Wymondley's and the Coronation Cup

LEST ANY RACING enthusiast be misled by the title of this article, let it be clear from the outset that it has nothing to do with a long-distance race run at Epsom during the Derby meeting!

At the northern end of Stevenage two roads lead northwards; the one on the west passes through Little Wymondley to Hitchin, while the eastern road goes through Graveley to Baldock. Travelling west from Baldock we can trace our way by the outskirts of Letchworth to Hitchin. Within this very roughly defined triangle lie the ancient manors of Much or Great and Little Wymondley.

These villages take their name from a Saxon whose name was Wymond, and the suffix 'ley' denotes that this was his pasture land. It is a curious characteristic of many of our ancient place-names that in speech they are very much abbreviated from the written word, and down to recent times some of the old inhabitants of the Wymondleys pronounced the name of these villages as Wimley.

In the time of Edward the Confessor the greater part of Great Wymondley was held by the church of St. Mary of Chatteris in Cambridgeshire, but in 1063 Earl Harold, later King Harold II, annexed the manor to the neighbouring royal manor of Hitchin.

Some twenty years after the Conquest, Great Wymondley was assigned to a Norman called Guy (Guido) Fitz Tecon. He held the manor by the feudal tenure of grand serjeantry and the condition of the tenure of Great Wymondley was that the lord of the manor offered the king his first cup of wine at the coronation banquet. The silver-gilt chalice used for this service was then handed back to him as his fee. This custom continued for over 700 years and was carried out for the last time at the coronation of George IV. William IV refused to have a coronation banquet, and as it has never been revived, this ancient ceremony has now lapsed.

William Alington, a descendant of Sir William Alington, who succeeded to the manors by his marriage to Elizabeth Argentine, presented the cup at the coronation of Charles II. This Elizabeth Argentine was herself a descendant of the family of that name who held the manor from before the end of the thirteenth century until the reign of Henry V, when the male line died out.

William Alington succeeded to the Irish peerage (Alington of Killard) given to his father by Charles I. He himself received the English barony of Alington of Wymondley from his monarch, Charles II. The manors were to remain in the Alington family for nearly 300 years. When William Alington died his son Giles succeeded to the manors at the tender age of eleven.

The ceremony of the coronation cup could not be performed by a woman, so as Giles was a minor the rite was performed at James II's coronation by his uncle Hildebrand, and at the coronation of William and Mary it was carried out by another kinsman, Sir John Jacob.

Hildebrand inherited the Wymondleys and the Irish peerage from his nephew, but soon afterwards sold the manors to Elizabeth, the daughter of John, Lord of Culpeper. At Queen Anne's coronation another male deputy was required to present the cup, and in this case it was Elizabeth's son William. However, in 1704 Hildebrand bought his inheritance back and he remained in possession until his death in 1723, when the Irish peerage also died out.

Great and Little Wymondley then came to be divided among his three nieces, Juliana, Viscountess Howe, Diana, wife of Sir George Warburton, and Catherine, wife of Sir Nathaniel Napier. Diana's daughter, also called Diana, married Sir Richard Grosvenor, baronet, of Eaton Hall,, Cheshire, who is said to have presented the traditional cup of wine at George II's coronation. Sir Richard eventually purchased the rest of the estates from his wife's kinsfolk and his nephew Richard was created Baron Grosvenor of Eaton in 1761. He thus received the first of a series of peerages, culminating in 1874 when his direct descendant in the male line became the first Duke of Westminster.

In 1767 Lord Grosvenor sold the manors to the Hon. Mordaunt Cracherode, who had sailed round the world with Lord Anson. He was succeeded in 1773 by his son, the Rev. Clayton Mordaunt Cracherode. As well as being a well-known collector of books and prints he was a numismatist and by his will left his various collections to the British Museum. He is said to have been of such a retiring nature that his dread, lest he should be called upon to execute the office of cup-bearer, embittered his whole life.

As the next coronation, that of George IV, was not to take place until 1821 and Mr. Cracherode died in 1799, if this story is true he worried himself unnecessarily and, like so many of us, hastened to meet his troubles halfway.

His sister Anne, who succeeded him, was a maiden lady about eighty years old. She enjoyed her inheritance for only a short time and by her will left her estates to the Rev. Shute Barrington, Bishop of Durham, in trust for sale.

From him William Wilshere, of The Frythe, Welwyn, purchased the estates in 1806 and in 1821 presented the cup of wine to George IV at his coronation. This was the last time that this ancient rite was carried out and, as Cussans tells us in his *History of Hertfordshire*, William IV's refusal to have a coronation banquet deprived William Wilshere's nephew and namesake of two of these silver-gilt goblets, as he would later have also officiated in the same capacity at Queen Victoria's coronation.

After him there succeeded in turn his brother Charles Willes and the latter's three unmarried daughters, Edith, Everilda and Alice. Alice died in 1934 and the succession then came to their cousin, the late Captain Gerald Wilshere. He possessed the cup presented to George IV but today no one knows the whereabouts of the Coronation Cup.

Kylin Archive

The Battle of Barnet

Richard Nevil,
Earl of Warwick
Kylin Archive

SEVERAL of the many different tales that are told of the battle of Barnet have one feature in common — an association with oak trees. This is, of course, oak country: Hadley Wood is still there as evidence of the fact, and probably 500 years ago there were more oak woods in the vicinity. Although the actual battle was largely fought on what was even more open ground to the west of the present wood, the Earl of Warwick — in the words of Warkworth's chronicle — 'lepte on horse-backe, and flede to a wode by the felde of Barnett, where was no waye forthe; and one of Kynge Edwardes menne hade espyede hyme, and one came uppone hym and kylled hym, and dispolede hyme nakede.'

It has been conjectured that the wood in which he was thus caught — as another early chronicler put it — 'somewhat fleinge' lay in what is now Wrotham Park, where relics of the battle have been found. But on a house called The Hermitage which faced Hadley Common until it was demolished a century ago there was an inscription to the effect that Warwick met his end under an oak tree that stood in front of it. The tree was generally known as Warwick's oak, though on some old picture postcards, it was referred to as the King Edward IV oak, that king being the victor of the battle. Well into this century the stump of it was to be seen, protected by railings, on the south side of the bridleway near Hadley church, though there is no trace of it left today.

This ancient oak has been identified with the 'gaunt leafless tree' from which Adam Warner was hanged in Bulwer Lytton's novel *The Last of the Barons,* even though the author admitted this episode to be purely imaginary. But he wrote a more circumstantial account — which also contains a reference to oak trees — of Warwick's last stand; according to Lytton when urged to 'fly through the wood' he spurned the idea and stood his ground. 'Behind the column which still commemorates the great battle of that day,' wrote Lytton, referring of course to Hadley Highstone, 'stretches now a trilateral patch of pasture-land. . . At that time this space was rough forest ground, and where now, in the hedge, rise two small trees . . . rose then two huge oaks, coeval with the warriors of the Norman Conquest. They grew close together, yet, though their roots interlaced, though their branches mingled, one hand had not taken nourishment from the other. They stood, equal in height and grandeur, the twin giants of the wood. Before these trees, whose ample trunks protected them from the falchions in the rear, Warwick and Montagu took their last post.'

For all the care that Lytton took to set the scene, however, *The Last of the Barons* is not to be relied on as history. But a book written by William Bullein in 1564 and called *A Dialogue against the Fever Pestilence,* though imaginary, has in it a reminiscence of the battle of Barnet — again involving an oak tree — that could possibly be founded on fact. In this a traveller crossing what from the description is clearly Hadley Green remarks: 'Here was foughten a fearfull feeld called Palme Sondaie battaile.' It must be admitted that the fact that the battle was actually fought a week later, on Easter Day, sows the seed of doubt about the authenticity of the anecdote that follows. It comes from Roger, the servant, who says: 'If it please your maistership . . . my graundfather was also here with twentie tall men of the Parishe where I was borne and none of them escaped but my graundfather onely . . . I heard my Grandame tell how he escaped.'

'Tell me, Roger, I praie thee,' says his master obligingly, 'how he did escape the daunger?'

'Sir,' replies Roger, 'when the battaile was pitched and appointed to be foughten neare unto this Windmill, and the Somons given by the Harottes of Armes, that Speare, Polaxe, blacke Bill, Bowe and Arrowes should be sette at worke the daie followyng, and that it should bee tried by bloudie weapon, a sodaine feare fell on my Graundfather; and the same night, when it was darke, he stale out of the Erles campe for feare of the kynges displeasure, and hid hym in the Wood; and at length he espied a greate hollowe Oke Tree with armes somewhat greene, and climbed up partly through cunnyng, for he was a Thatcher, but feare was worthe a Ladder to hym; and then by the helpe of a writhen arme of the Tree he went doune and there remained a good while, and was fedde there by the space of a Monethe with olde Ackornes and Nuttes whiche

Squirrels had brought in, and also did in his Sallet keepe the Raine water for his drinke.' His sallet was the headpiece of his armour; and thus, concludes Roger, he 'at length escaped the daunger.'

His master merely observes dubiously 'I never read this in the Chronicle,' to which Roger replies 'There be many thinges (and it shall please your Maistership) whiche are not written in the Chronicles, I do think are as true.' This one, however, sounds a rather tall story and leaves one wondering why it was necessary for Roger's grandfather to stay in the tree for a month after the armies had dispersed! Was it true, even though not written in the chronicles, was it a tradition, or was it a mere fabrication?

Tradition and truth, fact and fiction about the battle of Barnet seem to be as inextricably entangled as Warwick was — or so some say — in the wood. Perhaps it was the mist in which the battle was fought that, by preventing the combatants from seeing what was happening, created the confusion which has existed ever since and will probably never be entirely resolved. It seems that, as Holinshed wrote of the death of the Earl, of Warwick, 'we maie beleeve as we list' and can accept as much of this oak lore as we choose without fear of contradiction.

Kylin Archive

Field of battle near Barnet

Mother of 39 children

According to the *Guinness Book of Records* the British record for the greatest number of children borne by one mother is held by a Hertfordshire woman — Elizabeth Greenhill, of Abbot's Langley. She is said to have lived roughly between 1615 and 1679, to have married William Greenhill at the age of sixteen, and between 1631 and 1669 to have borne him thirty-nine children — thirty-two daughters and seven sons.

Let no sceptic dismiss this as impossible, for the world record is sixty-nine children — though it is only fair to add that this family was made up of sixteen pairs of twins, seven sets of triplets and four sets of quadruplets, which entailed a mere twenty-seven confinements. There were no such short cuts to fame for Elizabeth Greenhill, who had thirty-eight confinements, only two of her progeny being twins. This averages out at one confinement for every year of her married life, for she had her first child when she was about sixteen and her last, after her husband had died, when she was about fifty-four — which again is not impossible, for the Guinness book records two other mothers of that age and one of fifty-seven.

These were fairly recent and well-authenticated cases, but to verify Elizabeth Greenhill's family three centuries after the happy events is no such easy matter. Unfortunately, for the years when her children were baptized the Abbot's Langley parish registers are missing. On what evidence, then, does this tradition rest? A correspondent to the *British Medical Journal* in 1883 described it as 'a somewhat remarkable, well-authenticated instance of fecundity,' adding that 'the lady was of good position' and that all her thirty-nine children lived to attain their majority. This latest statement is very suspect, and its source is not quoted; the rest of his information the writer might have found in several publications. Perhaps the most likely is *Notes and Queries* for 1878, where mention is made of a portrait of Mrs. Greenhill with an inscription on the reverse.

At one time there were two such portraits. On the one that has survived the note on the back records that 'Mrs. Greenhil . . . had thirty-nine Children by one Husband; they were all born alive and baptized, and all single Births save one; the last Child who was born after his Father's decease was a Chirurgeon, and liv'd in King Street Bloomsbury, and wrote a Book of the Art of embalming human bodies.' Inside one copy of this book, incidentally, this statement was found repeated almost word for word. The note on the back of the portrait, however, adds more: it is attested by 'Richd Ashby,' a clergyman who claimed to have been 'well acquainted' with 'a credible Person' who had heard Mrs. Greenhill say 'that she believed if her Husband had lived she might have had two or three more Children.' Beneath his name appears a further note, in the same hand, that 'there was an Addition made to the Arms of the Family, to commemorate this extraordinary case.'

This addition to the Greenhill arms was made at the instance of the youngest and posthumous child, who was called Thomas. As a surgeon he had attended the earl-marshal, and to him in July 1698 he wrote:

'To his Grace Henry Duke of Norfolk, Earl-Marshal of England.
The humble Petition of Thomas Greenhill your Grace's Surgeon Humbly Begs That in consideration of your Petitioner's being the Seventh Son and Thirty-ninth Child of one Father and Mother your Grave would be pleas'd to Signalize it by some Particular Remark or Augmentation in his Coat of Arms to transmit to Posterity so Uncommon a Thing
And your Petitioner shall every pray, &co.'

With his petition he submitted a drawing on vellum of the arms as he wanted them altered. The earl-marshal admitted his claim to be the 'Nine and Thirtieth Child by Birth of the said William by Elizabeth his wife daughter of John Jones of London;' and, 'being well satisfied of the Qualifications of the said Thomas Greenhill and willing to gratify him in this his humble Request in consideration of his Services to me and my Family and to commit to Posterity the Memory of so Uncommon a Birth,' he granted Thomas's request. The grant of arms provided

The only surviving portrait of Elizabeth Greenhill

that 'the Arms born and used . . . by his said Father . . . may be allowed and confirmed to be born by him with ye Alterations of ye Barrs from Argent to Ermine, and whereas they have borne for their Crests in seals and otherwise a Demi-Griphon, he may be allowed to bear ye same Gules, powdered with thirty-nine Mullets or.'

A mullet in heraldry is a device in the shape of a star; the reason for their number is obvious. The difficulty, however, of depicting so many in such a limited space proved too much for the artist who drew the crest in the original grant in the College of Arms: he managed to get in only fifteen. It also defeated the Mr. Berchet who incorporated Thomas's arms in the frontispiece of his book *The Art of Embalming*, which was published in 1705. As a corrspondent to *Notes and Queries* commented, 'What an enormous demigriffin must be painted to make room for powdering him with thirty-nine mullets. This seems past all *bearing*' (his italics).

The story of the prolific Elizabeth Greenhill's family thus rests on the claim of her son Thomas to be her thirty-ninth child, but it can hardly be open to doubt if it was accepted by the whole hierarchy of the Heralds' College. Although Thomas was the earl-marshal's surgeon and also the friend of his herald, Blanche Lyon, neither would have endorsed a statement about his family unless he was safisfied that — to the best of his knowledge at least — it was true.

Besides, Thomas's is not the only statement about the number of his parents' children: one of their grandchildren, Thomas's nephew Joseph Greenhill, also put it on record. He was a clergyman who published a number of sermons, including one on 'The Presumptions and Sinful Practice of Inolculation,' but what is more to the present point is that he also wrote 'William Greenhill my grandfather was a Counsellor-at-Law, and Secretary to General Monk, lived at Abbots Langley in Hertfordshire, where his Family had long resided.' They had originally come from Greenhill Grove Harrow, but in 1612 William's grandfather had purchased Hyde Manor at Abbots Langley. His grandson William, went on Joseph, 'had by his Wife 39 Children all of whom died young except 4 Sons and 2 daughters.' He did not give the names of the daughters, but the sons who survived were called William, John, Henry and Thomas. Of these, Thomas's achievements have already been mentioned; the careers of the others are known from a family tree in the College of Arms. William, who was Joseph's father, followed in his own father's footsteps and became a counsellor-at-law;

John was a stationer; Henry 'went to the East Indies and there died.'

Sir Henry Chauncy, in his *Historical Antiquities of Hertfordshire* (1700), included a third daughter and stated — in error, it seems— that their mother's maiden name was White. By her, he wrote, her husband 'had issue William, John, Henry, Thomas and Elizabeth, Katherine and Anne'; of those who died young he made no mention. Elizabeth married a Mr. Dillingham, and either Katherine or Anne the Rev. Richard Ward. Both he and 'Mrs. Elizabeth Dillingham' appear in the list published in *The Art of Embalming* of 'such Noblemen and Gentlemen as have been pleas'd to Encourage this Work by Subscriptions,' as do also 'William Greenhill, Esq., for 3' and 'Mr. John Greenhill.' Perhaps one of William's three copies was for the absent Henry and one for a third — possibly unmarried — sister.

If the story had been true that all thirty-nine children attained their majority it would have been almost as remarkable as the fact of their birth. Those of the Abbot's Langley parish registers which have survived from the seventeenth century, like those of other parishes, are full or records of infant burials, and it seems that the Greenhills were not, after all, immune from this affliction. Perhaps the 'presumptuous and sinful practice of inoculation' might have saved them, but as it was the long-suffering Mrs. Greenhill, it seems, saw the burying of some thirty-two or thirty-three of her children — in itself something of a record.

Still, the fact that most of them died young does not really affect the issue — apt expression! Elizabeth Greenhill's claim to fame rests on her having given birth to so many; and as it has won her a place in the *Guinness Book of Records* it cannot be said to have been entirely labour in vain.

Highwaymen's Highway

'I PUT THE GOLD IN MY BOOTS and prayed unto the Lord to protect me,' wrote Robert Woodford in his diary on June 21, 1638, recording how he set off from London and, to his immense relief, 'came safe to St. Albans.' What made this such an adventure was the risk of highway robbery, for which the St. Albans road was notorious. No matter what time of day you travelled along it, it seems you were liable to be waylaid: it was at dawn that one William Symonds, in 1647, was robbed near South Mymms of the packet of money which he had been commissioned to take to London.

For the highwayman both the time and the place were propitious — the place because here was an increasingly busy, yet not too crowded, road with plenty of cover by the wayside: the time because the Civil War was conducive to lawlessness. And when the Commonwealth was established, many Royalists — like 'Captain' James Hind — turned for a living to highway robbery. In 1649 the Rev. Adam Martindale, not daring to travel along the St. Albans road on his own, waited in London 'for company to come safely downe with, for there was great robbery by the way.'

A proclamation issued in that same year by General Fairfax to the Commanders of the Army to apprehend highwaymen, far from daunting them, seems to have provoked them to further outrages: during the following week, in the space of two hours, twenty members of Captain Hind's gang committed forty robberies near Barnet. It was this, in all probability, that prompted Parliament a few weeks later to offer a reward of £10 to anyone giving information that led to the apprehension of a highwayman. Yet their numbers increased: hard-up young gentlemen found highway robbery an easy way to refill their pockets. Such a one

Hertfordshire Record Office

The Trwe Effigies of James Whitney, the Notorious Highwayman.

was the 'son of Sir Thomas Eyton,' who in October 1657 'fell into company with as mad blades as himself and upon the highway on this side of St. Albans . . . robbed a coach.' Young Eyton also killed a man and ended up in Newgate — 'A sad business.'

Whether this was the St. Albans-London coach, which had been running for some twenty years, or the first long-distance coach (to Chester), which had been introduced that summer, is not known: but all brought grist to the highwaymen's mill. They made the most of the opportunities provided by the delays caused by floods at Mymms Wash and the ascent of Ridge Hill, which was often achieved only by stopping to attach extra horses lent to each other by the waggoners.

After the Restoration in 1660 the Royalists found more legitimate employment and the casual highwayman was less often encountered on the road; instead highway robbery became more and more the work of a highly organised gang. In February 1669 it was reported that 'On Saturday last 5 Carriers had their Packes cutt betwixt St. Albans and London.' Three of them, who had come from Coventry, had lost goods 'to a considerable vallue, one of their Horses became quite taken away, & not yet heard of.' The report went on 'some others of that gang have bene seene in severall places . . . & continue still in these parts, but none dares seize them, they are so vigilant & well armed in so much that they have Rode through severall townes openly without Controule.' Was it they who were the four still at large, from a gang of twenty-four, for the capture of whom a reward of £20 was offered in November 1669?

The 'Glorious Revolution' of 1688, which brought William III to the throne, left many who felt no allegiance to that monarch: and some of these swelled the ranks of the highwaymen. Chief among them was 'the Jacobite Robber,' the self-styled Captain James Whitney. Born in Stevenage, he had kept an inn in Cheshunt before he was persuaded by a customer to take to the highway. His first robbery is said to have taken place 'within two miles of St. Albans,' where 'he encountered a Jolly Red-fac'd Son of the Church bravely Mounted.'

'Reverend Sir,' said the Captain, 'the gentlemen of your coat have long enough, in all conscience, preached up the edifying doctrine of Passive Obedience and Non-resistance, & now I am fully resolved to try . . . whether you are able to practise it. therefore, worthy Sir, . . . make no opposition, I beseech you, but deliver up the filthy lucre you carry about you.'

This consisted of 'Six score and ten guina's cloas'd up in the Wastband of his

Breeches,' which Whitney 'eased him of' — though 'not without a good deal of Expostulation.' He then 'sent his Horse home before him, to prepare his Family' and 'left him a all alone to his Contemplations in an adjoining Wood.'

The most improbable detail of this anecdote is the sequel, in which Whitney gave away four or five bags of his swag to a poor clergyman he met a mile and a

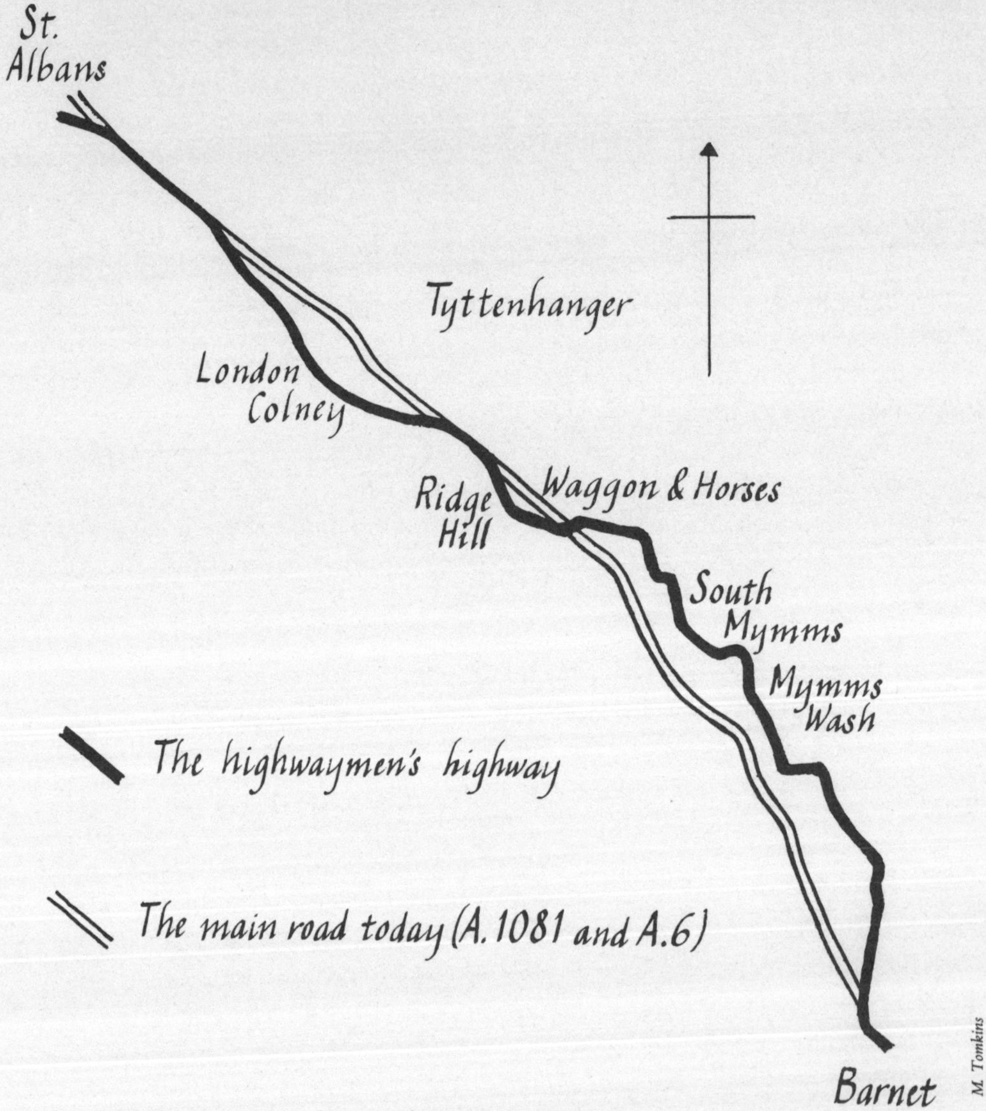

half further on. Whether it is true or not, however, a contemporary account leaves no doubt that 'The Road between Barnet and St. Albans was the usual Scene where our bold Adventurer play'd . . . his Frolicks': and there is a tradition that it was from the inn which was the predecessor of the Waggon and Horses, at the top of Ridge Hill, that his gang — some thirty strong — operated. One of them, perhaps, was the unsuccessful highwayman who was buried at South Mymms in 1689.

Whitney was not above burglary, as a butcher who lived near Barnet discovered to his cost after he 'Swore, by way of Bravado, that he had New-milled Crown-Pieces enough at home to pave the way between Barnet and St. Albans.' But most of our gallant captain's exploits took place on the highway, though not all on the St. Albans road. On November 14, 1691, for instance, he and three of his gang committed two robberies elsewhere in Hertfordshire: but even so, when their victims pursued them, it was to their old haunts that they fled. Perhaps they were heading for the inn on Ridge Hill when, 'in a Lane between Sir Thos. Pope Blunt's and Barnet, the Country-Men got up with the Robbers.' Sir Thomas' house was Tyttenhanger, just off the St. Albans road: and here Whitney and his colleagues shot his cook, a farmer and six horses before they made their escape.

It was probably Whitney's gang at work again on August 23, 1692, when 'the earle of Marlborough was mett by some highwaymen on horseback, near Coney, as he was goeing to his country house.' This was Holywell House in St. Albans, which he reached the poorer by five hundred guineas, while the gang 'made their escape.' Most likely this encounter was the result of Whitney's having 'constantly good Intelligence brought him of all the considerable Sums of Money that were ventured abroad.'

It was by this means that 'he came to be informed that a large Parcel of the King's Money was secretly put up in one of the Carriers Packs in Order to be transmitted to London, with less Expence.' The Manchester carrier who had been entrusted with this tax-money, seeing safety in numbers, set off early in November 1692 in the company of a number of lace-men. But he reckoned without Captain Whitney, who — with some seven of his gang 'disguised in Vizards' — lay in wait for him at 'South Mims-Wash.' First, however, they 'stopt all Travellers on the Rode . . . guarding them in a field,' while their horses were 'pounded . . . in a corner of the Lane. Having taken this precaution against interruption, they waylaid the convoy, robbed the lace-men and killed their horses, 'then nimbly examined the Carriers Packs and took out Seven Hundred Pounds. 'Before they called it a day they had secured £15000 and, 'when the exploit was don. & the Treasure taken, killed all the Horses of those they had stay'd, to hinder the pursuit of them: 16 Horses they stabbed & then dismiss'd those that they had dismounted.' And off they rode, 'our illustrious Captain . . . shaking a Hundred Pound Bag over his Head' and crying: 'This is a fine trade, my merry boys, if it will but last!'

For him it was not to last long, though he enjoyed a brief heyday. The London Gazette advertised in vain 'a considerable Sum of Money' stolen 'at Mimms-wash,' as well as a horse stolen on the same day 'by highwaymen between Barnet and South Mymms' — probably also Whitney's work. He again most likely organised the eight or nine highwaymen who robbed a waggon near Barnet in the same month and made off with between £1500 and £2000. By December there was 'noe travelling the roads' — until dragoons were posted about ten miles out of London on all the main roads. On the 6th at Barnet they apprehended Captain Whitney, who — after killing one dragoon and wounding several others — was finally caught.

Now that 'the terror of all who travelled from London either northward or westward' (as Macauley called Captain Whitney) had been removed, it must have been hoped that there would be an end to such atrocities as his murders at Tyttenhanger and 'His Butchery of the poor Horses at Mimms Wash.' But still the robberies went on: on January 11, 1693, 'some highwaymen stopt 5 waggons on St. Albans road, which they drove out of the way, and took out of them a pack, wherein was a summ of money, which they carried off': and on the 25th '10 highwaymen robbed divers country men near Barnet, and used them barbarously.'

The measure passed in 1695 for 'impressing' the unemployed into the army rid the roads of several rogues: but the Treaty of Ryswich in 1697 only disbanded them again, and back they flocked to their old trade. By October the Hertfordshire highways were again infested: and unemployment in 1698 made matters worse. The roads out of London were once more patrolled: and in 1699 anyone who secured the conviction of a highwayman was given not only a reward but a certificate exempting him from certain unpopular parish duties.

But neither these 'Tyburn Tickets' nor the setting up of the St. Albans and

South Mimms Turnpike Trust after 1715 spelt the end of highway robbery on this notorious stretch of road. The age-old collaboration between landlord and highwayman continued: since the latter spent 'full thrice as much in wine and beare' as his other customers (according to an ex-highwayman), the landlord to keep his custom — would often tip him the wink if any wealthy traveller stopped at his inn. Thus a St. Albans innkeeper in 1718, finding a visiting gentleman's portmanteau encouragingly heavy, introduced him to the highwayman Tom Garrett and his accomplice. With them the gentleman set off the next morning for London, but London Colney was as far as he got before they robbed him of the hundred guineas in his portmanteau and galloped away up a by-road. Thereupon he filled the portmanteau with stones and went back to the inn, where the landlord — finding it still heavy — assumed he had not after all been robbed. This disarmed him of any suspicions he might otherwise have had when the gentleman told him that, having enjoyed the company of the two men he had been introduced to, he would like to pay them a visit. The landlord gave him their addresses; and by threatening them, at their separate lodgings, with arrest — and a pistol — he retrieved a hundred guineas from each of them! Or so the story goes.

The highwaymen lurked in the valley-bottoms, according to a traveller who wrote an account in verse of a journey he made, through South Mimms to St. Albans, in 1733:

'Three bottoms here with danger I descend,
And every bottom gives a pistol'd fiend.'

But to rob and get away with it became increasingly rare as the century wore on; and the gibbet that stood on the St. Albans road after 1748 served as a grisly reminder of what happened to one who had robbed the Chester mail. The tables were now often turned on the highwayman: the South Mimms register briefly records the burial, in 1770, of 'William Ward, a highwayman shot in Mims Wash.' For travellers now took care to go well-armed: one, walking south from St. Albans when he was accosted by a footpad, turned a pistol on him and marched him to the cage at Barnet! The cutpurse of these latter days was a sad fellow compared with the swashbuckling rogue who had terrorised travellers on the St. Albans road in the 17th century.

Welwyn and the Frythe

AT THE SOUTHERN end of the old village of Welwyn and to the west of the London Road lies the extensive and well-wooded estate known as The Frythe. The name, which has remained unaltered through the centuries, is a Saxon word meaning 'wooded country' and gave its name to the earliest known residents, who were John de Frithe and John atte Frythe in the thirteenth century. In these days of mass development it is pleasing to note that the estate still retains its wooded character, and it is of interest to botanists because it contains a number of trees of various rare species, some of which are reputed to be the only known specimens of their kind in the country.

The present house, which was built in 1846, has a very pleasing and not too ornate exterior and contains a number of spacious rooms. One of these was for some time used as a private chapel, and until certain structural alterations were carried out a few years ago the following inscriptions could be seen under three lights of the east window:

HANC DOMUM REAEDIFICAVIT GULIELMUS
WILSHERE A.D. MDCCCXLVI.
(William Wilshere rebuilt this house A.D. 1846).

NISI DOMINUS AEDIFICAVERIT DOMUM
IN VANUM LABORAVERUNT QUI
AEDIFICANT EAM.
(Unless the Lord have built the house, they have worked in vain who build it).
HANC DOMUM AMPLIFICAVIT KAROLUS
WILLES WILSHERE. A.D. MDCCCLIII.
(Charles Willes Wilshere enlarged this house A.D. 1853).

Over a door in the south-west wall Queen Victoria's visit to Welwyn is commemorated by this inscription, in which the date appears in the form of a chronogram:

HAEC PORTA
VICToRIA PRIMA REGINA
AVLAE ADIVNCTA EST
(This door was added to the hall in the reign of Victoria I [*sic.*])

There are alternative versions of the date, of which 1844 seems the more likely. To the left and right respectfully of this door can be seen this welcome and farewell:

IN	EX
TRAN	EVN
TIBUS	TIBUS
SALVE	PAX
(Welcome to those entering)	(Peace to those departing)

During medieval times the estate belonged to the convent of Holywell in Shoreditch and was leased to the family of Wylshere or Wilshere, who had dwelt there since the time of Richard II. In the Record Office can be seen a lease made for sixty years from the feast of St. Michael 1523, which states that 'Dame Johanne Lynde prioress of the Monasterij of Saint John Baptiste of Holywell by London in the Countie of Middlesex and the convent of the same place leases to William Wylshere of the parish of oure blessed Lady of Welwyne in the Countie of Hertford yoman a tenement called the Boreshede which one Edward Swynnerton Gentilman late helde and occupied and another tenement called the frithe which standithe in a felde called Grigges felde and 50½ acres of land in the same parish.'

After the dissolution of Holywell Priory in 1539, The Frythe was granted to Sir John Gostwyke, Kt. and Joan his wife. Sir John died on April 15, 1545, and an inquisition taken at Ware on October 13 of the same year, confirmed that at the time of his death he was the rightful owner of the properties mentioned in the above lease, as well as thirty-four acres of pasture in Ashwell which formerly belonged to Thomas, Lord Crumwell and the advowson of St. Mary's, Welwyn.

This Sir John's son, William, died young and his brother, also named William, in 1546 conveyed the property to William Wylshere, who had formerly been a tenant of Holywell Priory. In view of the kaleidoscopic ecclesiastical changes of that troubled period, his will makes interesting reading. After expressing his desire to be buried in the family vault in the chancel of Welwyn church, he made a bequest to this church as well as to the churches of Codicote and Knebworth. He then left 10/- 'to the mendynge of the high waves betwyxt Wellwyn towne and Holmer hyll' leading to The Frythe. (This sum throws a vivid light on the depreciation of money since that date.) He further bequeathed money to poor maidens, poor men and priests for torches, burial dole and month tide, and after settling the bulk of his property on Thomas, his son, making a liberal provision for Joan, his second wife, and giving legacies to servants and others, four of whom were also named Wilshere but were not relatives, he gave 'to the parrysche churche of Wellwyne a syllver chalys upon condycyon that the curate of the said parrysh churche doo bid prayers for my sowll and Cicely my wiffes sowle every sonday in the pulpett when he doe bydd the beades.' As he died on November 15, 1558, which was two days before Queen Mary's death, it is most improbable that his pious intentions were ever carried out under the Elizabethan dispensation.

The long connection of the Wilsheres with the village of Welwyn and The Frythe is commemorated by a panel on the southern wall of St. Mary's, Welwyn, which tells us that members of the family had been interred there from the time of Richard II. The first of a list of ten who are mentioned individually is the William Wilshere who died in 1558, details of whose will are given above. The advowson of the church which he purchased in the time of Henry VIII remained in the possession of the family until it was sold by his great-grandson John to All Souls' College, Oxford, in the early part of the seventeenth century. His younger brother, Thomas, is numbered among the rectors of Welwyn and held the living from 1606 until his death in 1651. The last name on this panel is that of another William, who died in 1786.

This William's grandson, also named William, purchased the manors of Much and Little Wymondley in 1806.

The property eventually passed to the last named William's elder nephew, who bore the same Christian name, and he it was who built the present mansion in 1846. Dying unmarried, he was succeeded by his brother, Charles Willes, who

The ancient Manor House *F. Ballin*

not only enlarged the house but bore the greater part of the cost of rebuilding the chancel of St. Mary's in about 1865. He also built the Frythe chapel, now known as the chapel of St. Nicholas, on the south side of the church, and his name is commemorated in a chronogram on the exterior wall of this chapel. At Charles's death in 1906 The Frythe passed successively to each of his three unmarried daughters, who in their turn rendered great service to Welwyn by rebuilding the nave and tower of the church in the early years of this century.

Shortly after the end of the last war a large part of the house was leased to Imperial Chemical Industries Limited and research laboratories were erected in the grounds. This company purchased the freehold of the property at the beginning of 1955, and thus ended the Wilshere connection with The Frythe, which had spanned the greater part of six centuries.

During the Second World War the house was requisitioned for essential war work and a large hangar was erected in the grounds, in which the development and testing of mines and two-men submarines was carried out.

Until the Admiralty released the house in 1945, Captain Wilshere and his family lived in a house in the village.

In March 1963 Unilever Research Laboratories took over various parts of the house, which was henceforth shared between ICI and Unilever until 1964, when ICI withdrew their staff. Thereafter the Frythe was purely a Unilever Research Laboratory, where detailed research was carried out until most of their personnel and their work was transferred to Colworth House.

In May 1977 the house and grounds were bought by Smith Kline & French Laboratories Ltd. for their UK Research Institute.

Like Cussans in his erudite county history, we end our account of this fine old house with a Latin epigram attributed to Horace Walpole and applied to the Wilshere of his day:

UT DOMINUS DOMUS EST: NON EXTRA
FULTA COLUMNIS
MARMOREIS SPLENDET: QUOD TENET
INTUS HABET.

(A house is what its master makes it,
Outside columns count for nought,
Of marble splendid though they be,
What is within will claim your thought).

List of Subscribers

Aldenham School
Sir Peter Allen
Alleyne's School, Stevenage
Brian Anderson
Mr. and Mrs. Roy Arnold
D. G. Ashworth
Ruth Anthony
Miss. Gill Ayres
Enid Bailey
Peter and Sylvia Barker
Mr. and Mrs. David C. Barrett
Mr. and Mrs. Bartlett
P. Barton
Mrs. M. R. Bedford
Mr. and Mrs. Bennett
Beaumont School, St. Albans
W. H. E. Biddlecombe
Margaret Bowyer
Peter and Elizabeth Bull
Mr. I. F. Burns
Miss. Susan Burr
Mrs. W. Burr
Richard J. Busby
Mrs. Rose Caunt
Alan and Daphne Cheshire
Jeffrey Alan Clark
L. G. and M. A. Coburn
John Cole
Colney Heath and District L.H.S.
D. Cony
The County Record Office
Mrs. Jane Cotton
J. Coutts-Smith
L. S. Cox
Beryl Crawley
Tim and Heather Crichton
Michael A. Cuff
Norman C. Cuff
Alexandra M. Cullum
Philip D. Cullum
Mrs. Currey
Davids Bookshop
Mrs. B. N. T. Davies
Mr. and Mrs. Carl Davies
G. Davies
Mrs. D. J. Davis
Eric Stanley Dawkins
M. W. Day
Mr. and Mrs. Neville Deards
R. E. Dear
Marshall and Phyllis Dellar
Mr. and Mrs. Glyn Dimond
M. Dollimore
The Donalds
Alice and Colin Dunham
Mr. N. D. Elliott
K. E. C. Emsden
Charles Erwood
Joan Erwood
J. M. J. Estevez
M. M. Estevez
E. S. Kaulkner
M. J. Freeman
Doris Fuller
Miss. Elaine Gardner
Jack D. Garratt
Mrs. D. S. Garton
Mrs. Gillian Gear
H. L. Gearing
Mr. Huen Giddens
Mr. J. M. Goddin
Miss. R. M. Goddin
Ron Gough
Richard Graham
Henry W. Gray
Kenneth Green
Mrs. Sue Green
A. G. Greening
A. Greig
Mr. and Mrs. M. Guest
Mrs. M. Gullen
The Haberdashers' Aske's Boys School, Elstree
Dr. M. J. Hall
Mr. and Mrs. R. Halsey
Mr. C. W. Hancock
J. A. Harrison
Susan Harrison
Hatfield and District Archaeological Soc.
Mr. Adolph Hauke
Mrs. J. S. Hawes
Mr. and Mrs. P. A. Hawkins
Hemel Hempstead L.H. and R.S.
Mrs. D. M. Hemmings
D. J. Hillman

M. Hoather
Miss. Lynn Hodsdon
Mrs. E. Holden
A. G. Holloway
L. E. Hughes
Mr. and Mrs. Richard E. Hughes
Mary Hutchinson
Mr. Hunton Carter
Mr. and Mrs. Guy Johnson
Arthur Jones
Dr. Doris Jones-Baker
Mr. A. S. Joy
Mr. and Mrs. Eamon King
Mike and Val King
Mr. and Mrs. J. C. Kitchener
A. S. and N. K. Knapp
R. W. Knowles
Mrs. Jean R. Lange
C. L. Lee
Dr. and Mrs. I. Lenox-Smith
Mr. and Mrs. P. S. Lillie
George Lorimer
P. A. Magor
R. J. Magor
Mr. and Mrs. B. Maling
June McCready
Margaret Myddleton
Denis E. Miles
Mrs. D. R. Miller
J. B. Mills
Eric T. Moore
Mrs. I. Morris
Captain Richard Neall
Mr. and Mrs. A. W. Norman
Mr. B. Orza
Mrs. E. Orza
Ann Parker
Mr. F. J. Parker
Alan E. Payne
Mr. and Mrs. Pennington
Jo and Arthur Playford
Mr. and Mrs. D. C. Powell
Miss. M. G. Pritchard
J. M. Ragless
Mrs. J. Ricketts
Basil M. Roberts
Dr. Eileen Roberts
Gretta Roberts
Mr. K. J. R. Robson
Tony Rook
Peter Ruffles
Alan Ruston
The Marquess of Salisbury
R. M. Saunders
Sawtells of Sherborne Ltd.
Miss. M. D. Sayer
Mr. E. V. Scott
Colin Seabright
M. L. Steele
F. A. W. Steeley
Beryl Slater
Curtis Slater
Janet Slater
Irene and Edward Smith
Mr. L. E. Smith
Gill Simon
Mr. and Mrs. J. Sinclair
Dr. W. H. Taylor
T. Alex Thomson
Muriel T. Thresher
Simon and Gail Timothy
Mrs. Jessie Tomkins
Mr. and Mrs. S. Tomkinson
Mrs. D. G. Tomlin
Mr. and Mrs. G. Tomlinson
Laurie A. Tomlinson
Miss. M. V. Tomlinson
Peter and Alex Tucker
Miss. B. J. Turner
Turnford School
Verulam School, St. Albans
Dr. D. S. Wallace-Hadrill
Mrs. Anne Walsby
Andrew Wang
A. J. Ward
Miss. Evelyn M. Warner
F. G. M. Watson
J. Ware
Rev. C. A. Weale
Mr. H. J. Webb
J. Terence Wenham
A. F. G. Wheeler
J. T. Wheeler
S. E. G. Wheeler
Mrs. Pamela M. White
D. P. and T. J. Whitlow
Mr. F. Williams
Joan Williams
Dr. and Mrs. J. R. B. Williams
Alan Wilson
W. B. Winterton
G. P. Woods
I. D. Woolving
P. Wormleighton
Mr. S. A. J. Young

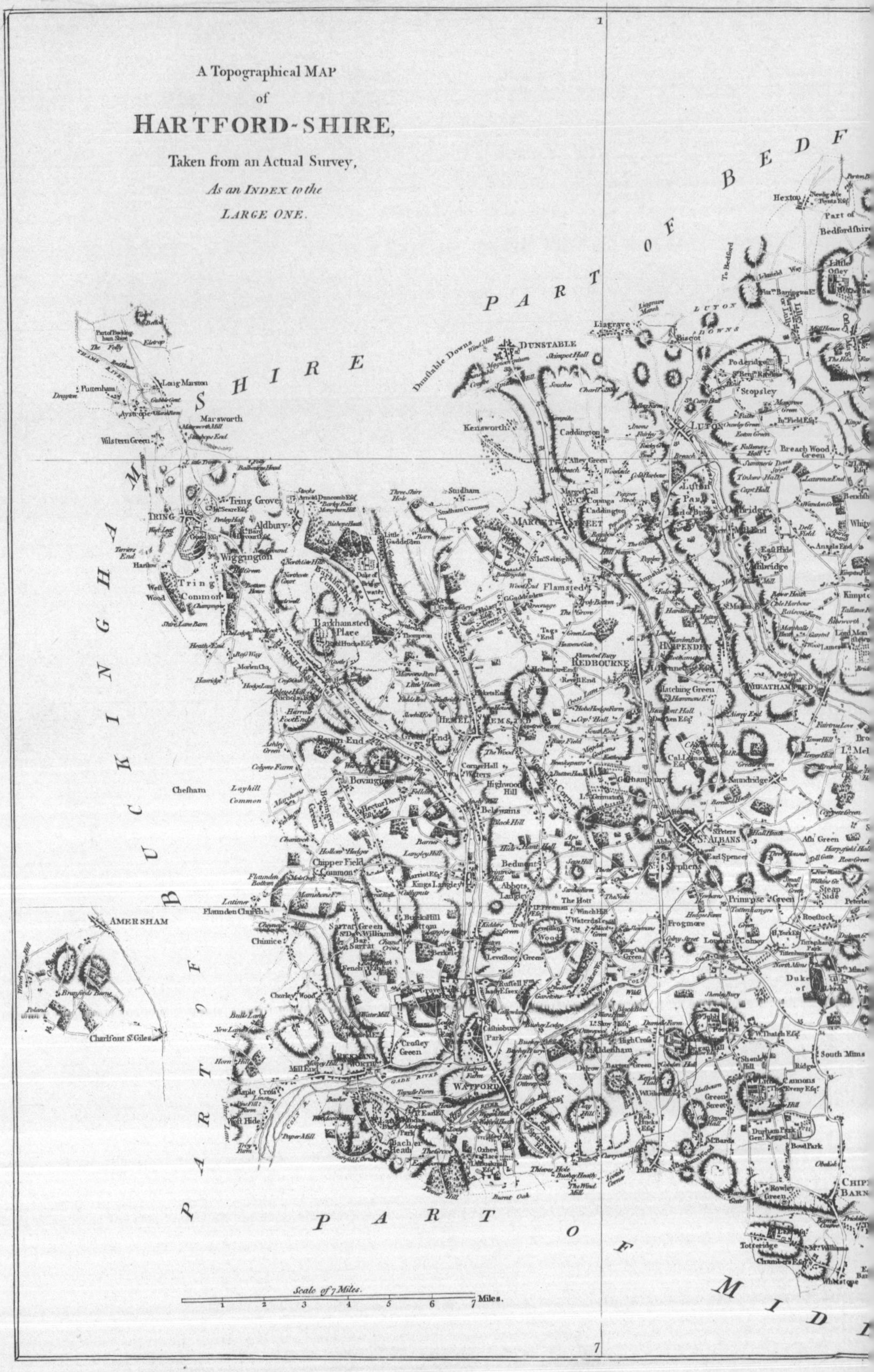
A Topographical MAP
of
HARTFORD-SHIRE,
Taken from an Actual Survey,
As an INDEX to the
LARGE ONE.
PART OF BEDF
BUCKINGHAM SHIRE
PART OF
PART OF MIDD
DUNSTABLE
LUTON
Hexton
Kensworth
Caddington
Tring Grove
TRING
Aldbury
Wiggington
Tring Common
Long Marston
Puttenham
Marsworth
Wilstern Green
Flamsted
REDBOURNE
HARPENDEN
WHEATHAMSTED
Berkhamsted Place
HEMEL HEMPS.
Bovingdon
Chesham
Layhill Common
Chipper Field Common
Kings Langley
Abbots Langley
Bedmont
ST. ALBANS
St. Stephens
Sandridge
AMERSHAM
Chalfont St. Giles
Latimer
Flaunden Church
Chinnice
Sarrat Green
Croxley Green
WATFORD
Cashiobury Park
Aldenham
Bushey
Primrose Green
Colney
London Colney
Ridge
South Mims
Shenley Hill
Totteridge
Whetstone
Stopsley
Breach Wood Green
Little Offley
Part of Bedfordshire
Scale of 7 Miles.
1 2 3 4 5 6 7 Miles.